Italy

100 Legendary Places

ROUGH GUIDES

Italy

100 Legendary Places

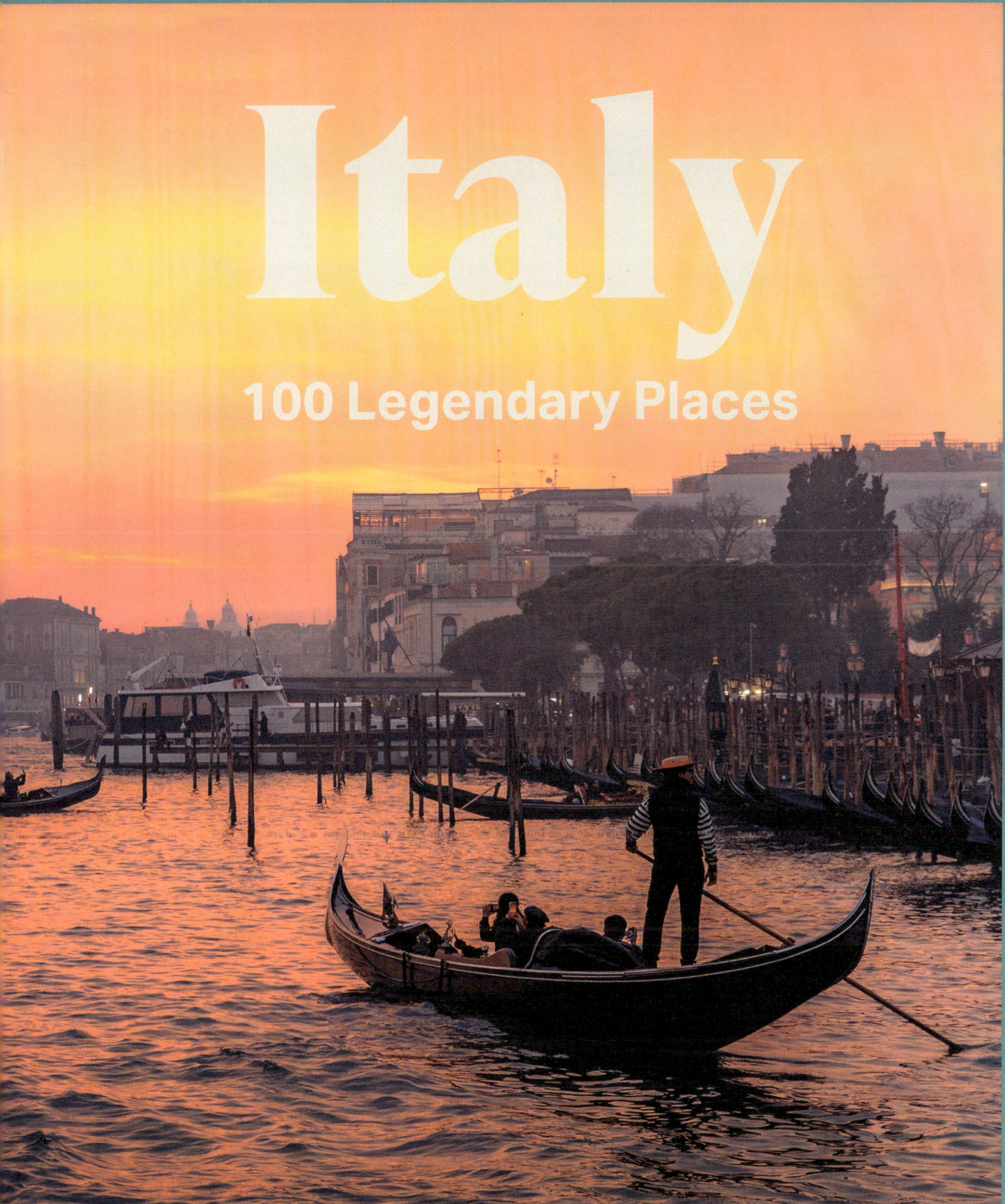

Italy
100 Legendary Places

Introduction

Italy barely needs introducing. Few countries are as powerfully, instantly recognisable – from Rome, with its ancient ruins and papal splendour, to Florence's Renaissance treasures and Venice, rising from the lagoon in stone and gold.

Yet the country's legend reaches far beyond these famous cities. It runs through the volcanic drama of Etna and the Aeolian Islands, the cliff-hung beauty of the Amalfi Coast, the Alpine lakes and Dolomite peaks of the north, and the ravines, caves and prehistoric stone towers of the south and islands. Smaller places evoke just as much wonder: Gubbio's medieval streets, Asolo's hilltop calm, Scanno's mountain traditions, Cividale's river gorge and the trulli country around Alberobello. Ancient worlds surface everywhere, from Pompeii and Paestum to Nora, Aquileia and Agrigento, while food, faith and landscape shape the experience as strongly as art and architecture.

This selection brings together the celebrated and the unexpected, the monumental and the intimate, inviting you on a journey through one of Europe's most richly varied – and indeed, legendary – countries.

Rome & Lazio

History's layers are proudly prominent in Rome, and the centuries pile up fast, with imperial avenues, papal treasures, Baroque fountains, neighbourhood markets and churches built over older worlds. Lazio loosens the frenetic grip of the capital with Ostia's ruins, Tivoli's villa gardens and Ponza's bright coves out in the Tyrrhenian, where crowded stone and piazzas give way to old ports, volcanic hills, island water and stretches of coast.

Rome's centro storico

(T) Piazza Navona is a UNESCO World Heritage Site

Ancient, theatrical, and charismatically worn, Rome's centro storico is where most visitors find the version of the city they've been longing for. Occupying a triangular chunk of land that bulges into a bend in the River Tiber, here Rome's heart beats outwards from densely-packed arteries of narrow streets and alleys that host some of the city's most striking classical and Baroque heritage, and its most vivacious street- and nightlife. Known as Campus Martius in the days of ancient Rome, back then the low-lying centro storico lay beyond the centre of the city, and was mainly occupied by barracks, sports arenas and temples, most notably the Pantheon. Later the core of Renaissance Rome, today its blend of crumbling piazzas and pallazzi, Baroque churches and fountains, blind alleys and streets buzzing with scooters and foot traffic epitomise the city's beguilingly contradictory spirit; it's a place feels at once sacred and profane, intimate and majestic.

Ancient Rome: THE Colosseum, Forum & Palatine

Representing Rome's ancient imperial core and mythic origins, the triumvirate of the Colosseum, Forum and Palatine hill still smoulder with a tangible sense of the city's status as the centre of the ancient world. Indeed, the Colosseum has long-served as a model for stadiums around the world. Having survived almost two thousand years of earthquakes, fires, riots, wars and plundering, it's as much a symbol of endurance as it is of imperial Rome. Nearby, the Forum, the beating heart of day-to-day life in Ancient Rome, with its sacred Temple of Saturn, Arch of Septimius Severus, Temple of Vesta, and House of the Vestal Virgins, retains a soulful atmosphere despite the crowds. Unhurried strolls along the cypress tree-shaded Via Sacra conjure a sense of the triumphal processions and sacred ceremonies that once played out on these stones. And all this overlooked by Palatine Hill, where Romulus is said to have founded Rome in 753 BC.

(O, L) In the Forum; (T) The iconic Colosseum

Vatican Museums & St Peter's

Built on the site of St Peter's tomb, the Basilica di San Pietro, better known as St Peter's, was worked on by the greatest Italian architects of the sixteenth and seventeenth centuries. On entering, visitors are greeted by the moving sight of Michelangelo's *Pietà*. Carved from a single block of marble, this graceful marvel depicts the Virgin Mary cradling the body of Jesus after the Crucifixion. Further inside, the church's vast dome is a time-stopping wonder, with Bernini's baldacchino, a 95-foot-tall gilded bronze canopy, also quick to catch the eye as it twists over the altar and tomb of St Peter. The Vatican Museums are no less impressive across a complex of spectacular galleries that showcase everything from ancient antiquities and classical sculpture, to High Renaissance paintings, with all roads leading to the Sistine Chapel, where the ceiling frescoes and painting of *The Last Judgement* on the altar wall reveal why they're among the most-viewed paintings in the world.

(L) The monumental St Peter's Square outside the basilica

Ostia Antica

Located at the mouth of the River Tiber, around thirty minutes by train from the city, Ostia Antica is the old port of Rome. In its heyday a thriving port city with a population of over 50,000, the oldest archaeological items unearthed here date back to the fourth century BC, and today the site is a mesmerizing place of ancient residences, baths, temples, taverns and trading offices that once served the commercial life of the empire. Oft-hailed the Pompeii of Rome, Ostia Antica's demise as a pivotal port and military outpost came about gradually, which means most of its structures, frescoes and mosaics are remarkably intact, as revealed on strolls along the Decumanus Maximus that still runs through a town that still ripples with a sense of everyday life in the ancient empire, thanks to its theatre, House of Diana, Mithraeum Baths, and an ancient café replete with counter, shelves and wall paintings.

(L) In Ostia Antica's ruins; (T) Terraced houses in medieval Borgo di Ostia Antica; (B) Ancient stone masks on pedestals

Tivoli

Located east of Rome in the scenic Sabine Hills, Tivoli has long served as a serene escape from the capital. Back in classical times, this was where wealthy Romans chose to retire. Later, well-to-do Renaissance families transformed the town into a theatrical place of villas, terraces, gardens and fountains. Taken together, Tivoli's two great UNESCO World Heritage Sites, Villa d'Este and Villa Adriana, encapsulate both eras with monumental impact. The sixteenth-century Renaissance Villa d'Este offers an abundance of terraced gardens and extravagant fountains, including the musical Fountain of the Organ. Inside, halls and apartments present a bedazzlement of fantastically detailed friezes and frescoes. Meanwhile, Villa Adriana, southeast of Tivoli, reveals the remarkable scale of Ancient Rome's devotion to imperial leisure. Once the private retreat of Emperor Hadrian, this sprawling oasis, built between 118 and 138 AD, includes the Maritime Theatre and stately Piazza D'Oro (Golden Square).

(O) Villa d'Este's Fountain of the Organ; (L) Statue at Villa Adriana; (T) More fountains as seen from Villa d'Este's terrace; (B) A disorienting spiral staircase inside

Ponza

Part of the volcanic Pontine archipelago, the tiny island of Ponza sits in the glittering Tyrrhenian Sea as a crescent-shaped oasis of natural beauty and old-time charm. Located halfway between Rome and Naples, Ponza's pretty harbour and main town casts an enchanting first impression. Here, a clutch of candy-coloured, flat-roofed houses are heaped above a pink semi-circle of promenade that curls around the harbour, where fishing vessels boats bob on crystalline water, and small boats wait to take visitors on trips to secret coves and nearby uninhabited islands. Just 8km long, and 2km across at its widest point, Ponza has little in the way of conventional showy tourist attractions. Rather, the island's allures lies in its raw magic: cliffs and coves, salty air and sublime sunsets. When the waves of Chiaia di Luna beach are too choppy, the clear, sheltered waters of the so-called Piscine Naturali near Le Forna are perfect for cooling off in at the end of the day.

(L) Ponza's harbour; (T) Natural framing of the landscape on Ponza; (B) Spaghetti cooked with the sea and land's produce

REALE

Piemonte & Valle d'Aosta

At Italy's northwestern edge, the mood is refined, borderland and Alpine. Turin sets the tone with Baroque order, museums and grand cafés, before the land softens into Alba's truffle country and the wine hills of the Langhe. Beyond Aosta, Roman remains and castles lead towards higher valleys, ski towns and Courmayeur, where Mont Blanc fills the horizon with snow, rock and clean mountain air.

Turin

Turin has a habit of surprising visitors who come expecting industry and latter-day polish, but find instead a city of tenderly renovated avenues and squares, opulent palaces, and splendid collections of Egyptian antiquities and Northern European paintings. Boasting a freshly-restored Baroque core, and a cornucopia of galleries and museums, Turin's cultural offerings are rich and satisfying, much like its 500-year-old chocolate tradition of blending local Piedmont hazelnuts with cacao. The city is also well-served by elegant pedestrian-only areas speckled with genteel Belle Époque-style cafés that evoke its literary connections. Rousseau, Ruskin, Nietzsche, Flaubert and Twain all enjoyed sojourns in Turin, and Primo Levi was born in here in 1919. With its broad boulevards, chic shopping arcades and grand royal palaces that formerly served as residences for the House of Savoy, the city almost evokes a Parisian vibe, but framed by the Alps, which are visible from the nineteenth-century Mole Antonelliana tower.

(L) A dazzling sunset over Turin's skyline

Sacra di San Michele

Steeped in myth and medieval faith, and accessed via a steep hike from the small town of Sant'Ambrogio, the 1000-year-old Sacra di San Michele is anchored on a rocky spur on Mount Pirchiriano. Offering sweeping views over the Val di Susa, this extraordinary religious complex first served as a Benedictine cultural hub, and later inspired Umberto Eco's 1980 novel, *The Name of the Rose*. This evocative murder mystery book was also turned into a film, starring Sean Connery. Climbing up to the forbidding fortified abbey and ascending the Scalone dei Morti (Stairs of the Dead) sets a suitably sombre tone, for it was here that the skeletons of monks were laid out for locals to pay their respects, and be reminded of their human frailty. On arrival, the zodiac-adorned entrance to the Gothic-Romanesque abbey church sparks a sense of mysticism that chimes with its location on the Sacred Line of St Michael, which connects seven shrines dedicated to St Michael, from Ireland to Israel.

(L) Sacra di San Michele at dawn; (T, B) The atmospheric remains of the abbey

Alba & THE Langhe

Gateway to the Langhe, a bucolic landscape where gastronomy, vineyards and hilltop villages have acquired near-mythic status among Italian food and wine lovers, the town of Alba is famous for delicate, aromatic white truffles, best paired with the region's seriously excellent reds. A place of red-brick medieval towers, Baroque and Renaissance palaces and quaint cobbled streets, Alba's late-Gothic Duomo stands proud and confectionery-pink on the central Piazza Risorgimento. Meanwhile, pretty shops along its main drag, Via Vittorio Emanuele II, offer the region's finest produce, including wines, truffles, cheeses, all manner of mushrooms, and *torta di nocciole* – a sticky, nutty cake. Beyond Alba, the hilly Vineyard Landscape of Langhe-Roero and Monferrato has been designated an Area of Outstanding Value by UNESCO, famed for making exceptional Barolo, Barbaresco and Barbera wines in line with ancient processes.

(O) Cattedrale di San Lorenzo, Alba; (L) Autumn falls over the vines in Langhe-Roero; (T) Local truffles adorn a pasta dish

Aosta

Surrounded by the Alps, Aosta is the attractive mountain-valley capital of Italy's Valle d'Aosta province. Offering access to the stunning valleys of the Parco Nazionale del Gran Paradiso, the ski resorts of Mont Blanc, and a sprinkling of fine castles, beyond being a gateway, Aosta has plenty to detain and delight history lovers. Founded in 25 BC as an imperial military camp, it boasts a bounty of mighty Roman ruins. In the east, the dignified Arco di Augusto celebrates the Roman victory over the Salassi, a tribe from the Italian side of the Little St Bernard Pass. Just beyond, the arch of a well-preserved Roman bridge spans the dried-up River Buthier. Meanwhile, the Porta Praetoria, one of the town's most impressive sights, lies to the west. These imposing parallel triple-arched gateways once served as the main entrance into the Roman town. If that wasn't enough, Aosta's Teatro Romano was one of the few Roman theatres to have originally been roofed.

(L) Aosta's castles include Saint-Pierre; (T) Aosta's lively main street; (B) The Matterhorn is visible from the Valle d'Aosta

Courmayeur & Mont Blanc

(T) Courmayeur and Mont Blanc in summer

Sitting at the head of the Aosta Valley, beneath the great white mass of Mont Blanc, Courmayeur is the region's oldest Alpine resort. That said, Courmayeur is much more than a well-known resort name. Belonging to a valley system that sees roads and rivers snake towards the foot of Mont Blanc, passing castles, forests and villages shaped by snow, visitors flock here in winter for superb skiing in a majestic setting. Through the warmer months, hikers, climbers and mountain bikers arrive to enjoy the clean air and high routes. Excellent rafting and angling can also be enjoyed in the area, with the rotating, glass-fronted Skyway cable car offering a close encounter with Europe's highest mountain outside the Caucasus's. In fact, the terrace at the car's top station, Punta Helbronner, serves views of Mont Blanc, Monte Rosa and the Matterhorn. Just south of Courmayeur, Pré-Saint-Didier's thermal baths are on hand to soothe aching muscles after a day's skiing or hiking.

Liguria

A thin strip of land can pack in a surprising amount. Liguria squeezes ports, villages, terraces and railway lines between its steep hills and the sea, beginning with Genoa's palaces, medieval lanes and working harbour. Further east, Camogli, Levanto, the Cinque Terre and Portovenere cling to a coast studded with fishing boats, walking paths, vineyards and cliffs, all angled towards the clarion call of the water.

Genoa

(T) Arrivals in Genoa have long been made by sea

Melding maritime history with a thriving modern dockside district, Genoa straddles the apex of Liguria's arching coast, and marks the midway point of the Italian Riviera, dividing it into two distinct halves. Described by American-British author Henry James as "the most winding, incoherent of cities, the most entangled topographical ravel in the world", the city, one of the busiest in Europe, remains enticingly eclectic, vibrant and brimming with rough-edged style. With salt and trade etched into its bones, Genoa's nickname, "La Superba", still rings true on grand Via Garibaldi. Beyond the revitalized port, the old town is a tangled maze of medieval alleyways, with a series of large grand *palazzi*, built in the sixteenth and seventeenth centuries by Genoa's wealthy mercantile families, now transformed into museums and galleries that present the cream of Genoa's art collections, as well as furniture and decor from the grandest days of the city's past.

Camogli & THE Portofino headland

Located on the west side of the peninsula of Portofino, Charles Dickens experienced Camogli as the "saltiest, roughest, most piratical little place". While it still has the "smell of fish, and seaweed, and old rope", its rough edges have long been rubbed away, and it's now one of the most attractive resort areas along the Riviera di Levante. Its name, a contraction of Casa Mogli (House of Wives), derives from the days when women ran the port while men were away on voyages that lasted for years. In its heyday, Camogli supported a fleet of seven hundred vessels that once saw off Napoleon. Today, though, Camogli is a low-key Ligurian fishing village that's resisted the urge to turn itself into a tourist showpiece. Pressed hard against the coast, pretty houses rise above a small harbour and a curve of beach, with wooded slopes, sea cliffs and walking routes up the Portofino headland giving this stretch of coast rustic, and romantic, charm.

(O) Camogli's bell tower; (L) A home with an exquisite vantage point near Portofino; (T) Colourful buildings and seacraft in Camogli

Cinque Terre

Strung along the coast, the Cinque Terre (Five Lands) comprises five romantic hillside villages laced together by coastal hiking paths that overlook the shimmering Ligurian Sea. While each town – Monterosso, Vernazza, Corniglia, Manarola and Riomaggiore – has its own character, together they form a collective of candy-coloured clifftop communities that conceal labyrinths of medieval alleys and piazzas. Collectively, the towns also include a national park, a protected marine area, and a UNESCO Site of Outstanding Universal Value. While Vernazza is often considered the most picturesque village, with its natural harbour, small sandy beach, and distinctive tower houses, Corniglia is arguably the most romantic. The smallest and most remote village, access to the water and train station comes courtesy of an adorable staircase, and it's the starting point for a number of stunning hikes. The classic, and best, way to soak up the staggering beauty of the Cinque Terre is to follow the coastal paths, with flashes of cobalt sea drawing the eye from the tiny harbours below.

(L) Colourful Riomaggiore; (T) Vernazza's harbour; (B) Local lemons for sale

Levanto

Anchoring the westernmost point of the Cinque Terre, set just beyond the five villages, sea-facing Levanto is a delightfully unpretentious resort town that's long been loved by Italian families. Surrounded by pine forests, olive groves, and vineyards, Levanto is also markedly quieter and more affordable than its five more famous neighbours and boasts a bona fide seaside vibe that feels distinctly local. With a sandy beach actually in town (one of the biggest in the region, and good for surfing), and a beautiful, bijou medieval core of winding lanes and churches, it's an authentic base from which to explore the area, with several trails heading south to Monterosso, and more rugged coastal drama opening up to the east. The 6km cycle path to Bonassola and Framura is another highlight. Following the route of an abandoned railway track, brilliant-blue coastal views are served up between stretches through the old train tunnels.

(L) Boats on the beach at Levanto

Portovenere & THE Gulf of Poets

Sitting at the mouth of the Gulf of Poets, Portovenere exudes a divine beauty and confidence that befits its name, which means "Port of Venus". Affectingly serene, Portovenere's pretty waterfront is lined with rose- and yellow-painted tower-houses, packed tight above a picture-perfect marina, while the brooding thirteenth-century church of San Pietro, built over the ruins of a Roman temple to Venus (hence the name), stands on a rocky point overlooking the Ligurian Sea. In the main part of town, steps lead up from Via Capellini to the twelfth-century church of San Lorenzo, and higher to the remains of the sixteenth-century Castello Doria. Portovenere has also long carried literary connections, thanks to the rocky cove of Grotto Arpaia having been a favoured spot of Lord Byron. The poet swam from here to visit Shelley at San Terenzo across the bay, and to this day, the gulf is nicknamed "Baia di Byron".

(O) Portovenere's dazzling waterfront; (L) Castello Doria; (T) Alfresco dining; (B) Carved details adorn buildings

Lombardy & THE Lakes

Stylish Milan may be Lombardy's economic engine, but the region soon reveals itself as far more than fashion, finance and industry. Beyond the city lie Gothic spires, hidden courtyards and the enduring legacy of Leonardo, before the watery Renaissance serenity of Mantua and Bergamo's high-walled Città Alta. North of the plain, Lakes Como, Maggiore and Garda unveil another side of Lombardy: villa gardens, ferries, mountain slopes and elegant resort towns.

Milan

Milan might be Italy's powerful northern commercial hub, but this elegant, culture-rich city offers far more than business. History and artistic heritage reveal themselves in enticing layers, from the vast Gothic Duomo at its heart and the elegant Galleria Vittorio Emanuele II to the operatic prestige of La Scala and the imposing Castello Sforzesco. Leonardo's *The Last Supper*, painted on the refectory wall of Santa Maria delle Grazie, gave the world one of its most enduring images, while the Pinacoteca di Brera, housed in the Palazzo Brera, reveals the depth of Milan's artistic life through masterpieces by Raphael, Caravaggio, Andrea Mantegna, and a celebrated collection of twentieth-century art. Beyond its great monuments, the city's character unfolds in secluded courtyards, grand Fascist-era public buildings, lively neighbourhoods and stylish aperitivo bars, creating a destination where history, innovation and fashion coexist with effortless sophistication.

(L) Walking amidst the Gothic spires on the rooftop of Milan's Duomo

Mantua

The setting for Verdi's *Rigoletto*, and the place where Romeo heard of Juliet's supposed death, Mantua's seductive fictional credentials are more than lived up to by reality. Also hailed the most romantic city in the world by English writer and philosopher Aldous Huxley, Mantua radiates the dignified grace of a place that's fully aware of its former significance, and sustained allures, with a stylish skyline of domes and towers rising above its three encircling lakes. Fittingly, Mantua's history is characterized by operatic plot twists, most of them acted out by the Gonzaga dynasty. One of Renaissance Italy's richest and most powerful families, the Gonzaga ruled the town for three centuries, and their splendid Palazzo Ducale features Mantegna's fresco of the family and court. Today, Mantua's cobbled central squares retain a medieval aspect, and showcase remarkable architecture that ranges from the romantic medieval Rotonda di San Lorenzo, to the enormous Renaissance Basilica di Sant'Andrea.

(L) Mantua's Rotonda di San Lorenzo and clock tower; (T) Palazzo Te; (B) The eighteenth-century Biblioteca Teresiana

Bergamo Alta

With its steep streets flanked by high facades and encircled by sixteenth-century walls, Bergamo Alta, the upper town of a city of two halves, looks largely as it did in the Middle Ages. The lower town, Bergamo Bassa, is a more modern affair, with the two connected by a funicular railway. Enclosed by a harmonious miscellany of buildings, Piazza Vecchia sits at the heart of the upper area. The stage for joyous celebrations in 1797 – when the French formed the Republic of Bergamo and the square was carpeted with tapestries and transformed into an open-air ballroom – it's a magnificent place of wrought-iron-balconied houses, with the opulent Palladian-style civic library and imposing medieval Palazzo della Ragione. For breathtaking views of the old town and valley below, it's well worth climbing to the top of the twelfth-century, fifty-two-metre Torre del Gombito.

(O) By Cappella Colleoni in Bergamo Alta; (L) Fountain in Piazza Vecchia; (T) Bergamo is encircled by city walls

Lake Como

(T) The picturesque town of Varenna, Lake Como

Of all the Italian Lakes, it is the forked Lake Como that inspires the greatest devotion. The English Romantic poet William Wordsworth described it as "a treasure which the earth keeps to itself". Hugged by verdant mountains, with elegant villas, lush gardens and charming towns tucked between steep slopes and busy ferry routes, the lake stretches in a ribbon of deep blue seemingly lifted from a painter's sketchbook. Nowhere is this more apparent than in the neighbouring towns of Varenna and Bellagio: Varenna is celebrated for the lakefront botanical gardens of Villa Monastero, the medieval Castello di Vezio and the aptly named Riva Grande (Lovers' Walk), an ivy-clad waterside promenade. Across the water, picture-perfect Bellagio has long been regarded as one of Italy's most beautiful towns. Its lakeside promenade is lined with oleanders and lime trees, while neoclassical gardens, elegant fin-de-siècle hotels and flower-filled streets complete a setting of extraordinary beauty.

Lake Maggiore & THE Isole Borromee

Shared between Lombardy, Piemonte and Switzerland, Lake Maggiore is the epitome of old-time glamour, with the three breathtaking Borromean Islands (Isole Borromee) the lake's resounding leading attractions. Rising from the bay between Stresa and Pallanza, the islands transform the lake into a floating theatre of aristocratic elegance, with a microclimate responsible for their lush botanical beauty. On Isola Bella, Carlo III Borromeo's fantastical seventeenth-century residence showcases sumptuous Baroque gardens, while its opulent palazzo boasts a banqueting hall, ballroom, throne room, and grottoes adorned with mirrors. Over on the bigger, but less visited, Isola Madre, a sophisticated palazzo houses a collection of eighteenth-century puppets, and its gardens of azaleas, rhododendrons, palm and citrus trees host a colony of parrots. Closest to shore, Isola Superiore, commonly known as Isola dei Pescatori, is famous for its featuring in a scene in Ernest Hemingway's 1929 novel *A Farewell to Arms*.

(O) Elaborate garden statues on Isola Bella; (L, T) Borromeo's palazzo's elegant entrance and garden staircase; (B) Isola dei Pescatori from above

Lake Garda

The largest of the Italian Lakes, Lake Garda also possesses the most varied character across its ever-shifting landscapes. The lake is so large, in fact, that it alters the local climate – which is milder and sunnier than might be expected. Its narrow north is tightly enclosed by mountains that drop sheer into the water, with villages wedged into gaps in the cliffs, while further south, the lake expands. Lined with peaceful resorts, it's also flanked by gentle hills and olive- and vineyard-backed shores in places. Around its expanse, a wealth of castles, promenades, old resort towns and family-friendly beaches continue to give Lake Garda a broader appeal than its grander rivals. In the south, Desenzano is a delightfully cheery spot, and close to the scenically-impressive Sirmione, while the western shore is home to the lake's best destination, Gargnano, which offers a quieter, more authentic flavour of lake life, not to mention handsome Salò, with its intriguing history as the nominal capital of Mussolini's Nazi-backed puppet regime from 1943 to 1945.

(O) Sirmione's castle; (T) Pretty Limone's harbour; (B) Watching watersports on Lake Garda

Trentino-Alto Adige

In this northern corner of the country, Italy begins to speak with an Alpine accent. Trento and Bolzano blend frescoed streets, vineyards, museums and Austro-Hungarian echoes, while Germanic and Italian cultures meet in valleys of orchards and castles. Above them, the Dolomites rise in pale towers and jagged walls. The Brenta Dolomites, Pale di San Martino and Lago di Braies draw journeys into high trails, mountain refuges, mirrored waters and soaring rock.

Trento

(T) Panoramic view over Trento

Overshadowed by Monte Bedone, Trento is one of northern Italy's most appealing mountain cities, though it only became properly part of the country in 1919 after centuries of being hotly contested with Austria. Known as Tridentum to the Romans, a name celebrated by the eighteenth-century Neptune fountain in Piazza Duomo, Trento's old centre features frescoed facades, elegant arcades, and grand palazzi, which lend the city a dignity that feels distinct from both the Italian plain and the high Tyrolean valleys to the north. While stylish shops, boutiques and restaurants occupy the narrow streets that wend off the piazza, enormous moss-covered city walls lie beyond, and all this encircled by spectacular mountains, with the sixteenth-century Castel Toblino to the west of town, amalgamating the area's stand-out allures in one site. Located on a lush peninsula that stretches out into the Lago di Toblino, this enchanting mountain-backed lake fortress is steeped in local fairy legends.

Bolzano

Set between mountains and wine country, Bolzano (largely known by its German name, Bozen) straddles the jade-hued Alpine waters of the Talvera (Talfer) and Isarco (Eisack) rivers. Though the capital of Alto Adige, Bolzano has a tendency to feel more Austrian-Tyrolean than outright Italian. Indeed, it's a city that sees an Italian *La Dolce Vita* vibe sit shoulder-to-shoulder with traditional Alpine charm through its languages, food and mountains-meet-vineyard landscapes. Bolzano's heart can be found on Piazza Walther, where the striking Duomo di Santa Maria Assunta dominates views from pretty pavement cafés. World-renowned for the 500-year-old "Ice Man" displayed in its impressive Museo Archeologico, Bolzano's historic and architectural highlights run from prehistory through Gothic grandeur to twentieth-century Functionalism. Here, Piazza della Vittoria signals the end of Bolzano's German and Gothic quarter, and the beginning of its 1930s Functionalist zone, much of it laid out by Mussolini's favourite architect, Marcello Piacentini.

(L) Tyrolean archiecture in Bolzano; (T) Ice-cream colours on the buildings; (B) Reproduction of "Ice Man"

Dolomiti di Brenta

Northwest of Trento, the saw-toothed crests and glaciers of the Dolomiti di Brenta are among the wildest peaks in Trentino-Alto Adige. Traversed by less-trodden paths than the better-known Dolomitic peaks to the east, this is Italy at its most raw and physical. A place of jagged rock towers, high trails and pristine lakes, where landscapes are formed from ledges, spires and sudden drops, conjuring an intoxicating mix of drama and secrecy. Though steep, few peaks rise above 3000m, and the paths are easy to follow. While more serious climbers come here for the towers of Cima Tosa and Cima Brenta, accessible by via ferrata – iron "ladders" knocked into the rock – Val Genova offers a gentler beauty, with a woodland path winding past waterfalls that cascade down the mountains. More romantic woodland scenery can be found around the quiet lake resort of Molveno, with the Val Rendena offering verdant valley scenery, and pretty frescoed churches.

(O) Dolomiti di Brenta peaks; (L) Via ferrata traversing;
(T) A well-earned hiking pause with a view;
(B) Mountainsides in winter

Pale di San Martino

An otherworldly realm of pale pink-hued rock, lunar-esque plateaux and jagged silhouettes, the Pale di San Martino mountains form one of the most spectacular hiking areas in the Dolomites. Encompassing 240 square kilometres across eastern Trentino and Belluno, the range is part of a protected UNESCO World Heritage Site, and the largest mountain massif in the Italian Dolomites. Presently 2000 metres above sea level, the range was formed as a coral reef some sixty million years ago. Still today, white shells crunch underfoot on the trails, and the pale rock reflects bright slabs of light throughout the day. Sitting within the Parco Naturale Paneveggio, a vast area of ancient rolling woods and pastures laced by nature trails, campsites and ancient paved *reversi* paths, Pale di San Martino and its environs presents Alpine scenery at its sharpest and most dramatic.

(L) A spectacular rainbow over the high mountains

Lago di Braies

A spectacular deep-green lake surrounded by pines, Lago di Braies (also known as Pragser Wildsee) is suffused in the ancient folklore of the area's indigenous Ladin people. According to legend, the southern end of the lake, directly below the imposing peak of the Croda del Becco, serves as the secret gateway to the once-powerful subterranean Kingdom of Fanes, with other legends relating fantastical tales of witches, ogres, dragons, and a princess who appears on a boat when the moon is full and the mountains open. As such, it's clear why *Lord of the Rings* author J. R. R. Tolkien is said to have taken inspiration from the legend-steeped Ladin territory, and the wider Dolomites. The enchanting starting point of the multi-day Alta Via 1 hike that traverses the Parco Naturale Fanes-Sannes-Braies, Lago di Braies is easily accessed from the charming town of Dobbiaco (also called Tolbach), or else the glitzy Cortina d'Ampezzo ski resort, which brings to mind an Italian St Moritz.

(L) Imposing peaks over the forests and meadows; (T) Rowing boats on Lago di Braies; (B) Alpine-style resort

Venice & THE Veneto

Venice gives the Veneto its most unforgettable image: palaces rising from water, mosaic domes, lagoon islands and alleys that unsettle ordinary geography. Inland, the region opens into art cities, river bends, hill towns and cultivated countryside. Elsewhere, Padua holds Giotto's frescoes, Vicenza reflects Palladio's architectural grace, Verona curves along the Adige, and Asolo brings arcaded streets, villas and gardens to the foothills.

Venice

Rising from a humble mudbank inhabited by fishermen in the early Christian era, Venice has blossomed into one of the most visited cities in the world. While the crowds can be overwhelming, it remains an enchanting, dream-like realm that's likely to live up to most travellers' wildest dreams. It's fair to say that all the photographs you've seen of the Palazzo Ducale, Basilica di San Marco, and grand palaces along the Canal Grande have simply been recording the undeniable truth: Venice really is extraordinarily beautiful. Arguably, though, the City of Water's true beauty is to be found beyond the likes of San Marco, where canals narrow, and quieter corners and unnamed alleyways are as likely to hold works by Tintoretto, Bellini or Carpaccio as many of the major museums. A floating vision that appears almost as an order-defying miracle, Venice is at once fragile, theatrical, and the undisputed masked Queen of the Adriatic.

(L) Venice at sunrise

Venice lagoon islands

As well as offering ways to escape the city's dense throng of tourists, the islands lying to the north of Venice – San Michele, Murano, Burano and Torcello – are richly rewarding in their own right. Encased by tall red-brick walls and cypress trees, and blessed with Renaissance architecture, San Michele is Venice's dedicated cemetery island. Established by a Napoleonic decree, most Venetians lie here for about ten years, after which their bones are dug up and removed to an ossuary. While Murano's glass-making excellence needs no introduction and dominates visits to the island, it's also home to several stunning churches. Then there's Burano. Formerly a centre of traditional lace-making, these days the biggest impression left by this fishing-based island comes courtesy of its adorable, brightly painted houses, while scarcely-populated Torcello, known as the "Mother of Venice" as a result of being settled by refugees from the mainland in the fifth century, is home to Venice's first cathedral, Santa Maria dell'Assunta.

(L, T) Murano's colourful buildings; (B) A glassblower shaping molten glass with his tools

Padua

With its arcaded streets, lively markets, longstanding university heritage and present-day student population, Padua feels quite different from Venice's watery spectacle. A Roman municipium dating to 45 BC, it is one of the Veneto's oldest cities and has long been shaped by both scholarship and faith. Italy's second-oldest university was founded here in 1222, establishing Padua as one of Europe's great centres of learning. Under the fourteenth-century domination of the Da Carrara family, Padua's cultural eminence was secured, with Giotto, Dante and Petrarch among the notable figures who were attracted to the city. Today, Basilica di Sant'Antonio remains a major pilgrimage church, while Giotto's frescoes in the Cappella degli Scrovegni draw devotees of Italian art. At the same time, a large student population maintains a young, vibrant atmosphere.

(O) Cycling in the shadow of the Basilica di Sant'Antonio; (L) Fresco cycle by Giotto in the Cappella degli Scrovegni; (T) Youthful street life

Vicenza

Absorbed by Venice in 1404, Vicenza's abundant Gothic palaces reflect its status as a Venetian satellite, though in the latter half of the sixteenth-century the city was transformed by the work of an architect who owed nothing to Venice and was to influence every succeeding generation: Andrea di Pietro, alias Palladio. Today, much of Vicenza's centro storico looks much as it did when Palladio's buildings were constructed. The city's handsome, well-heeled heart is truly a place of Palladian treasures, among them the Palazzo Chiericati, now the home of the Pinacoteca di Palazzo Chiericati, where works by celebrated names such as Tintoretto, Giambattista Tiepolo and Van Dyck punctuate a picture collection dominated by Vicentine artists. Another highlight is Palladio's Teatro Olimpico, the oldest indoor theatre in Europe. Designed by Palladio, who died soon after work commenced, construction was overseen by Scamozzi. The theatre opened on 3rd March 1585, and is still used for concerts and plays today.

(O) Villa La Rotonda, a Palladian masterpiece, just outside Vicenza; (L) In the centro storico; (T) Venetian columns on Piazza dei Signori; (B) Detailed architecture in Teatro Olimpico

Verona

Cradled in the low amphitheatre that the wide River Adige has carved out of the hills, Verona is one of northern Italy's most handsome cities. With its Roman sites, ancient bridges, and streets of pink-hued medieval buildings, Verona also has more in the way of historic attractions than any other place in the Veneto except Venice itself, with the bonus that it's not overwhelmed by tourism. In addition, despite being the largest city of the mainland Veneto, Verona invites easy immersion: cars and buses are prohibited from many squares and medieval lanes in its historic centre. While Juliet's balcony at Casa di Giulietta does draw crowds, Verona's appeal is older and broader than the Shakespearean legend attached to it. Looming over Piazza Brà, Verona's Arena was the third-largest of all Roman amphitheatres, with its red-and-white-striped Duomo, and fourteenth-century Arche Scaligere market also revealing Verona's status as a place of venerable riverside romance.

(L) Fair Verona; (T) Bronze statue of Juliet at Casa di Giulietta; (B) A panoramic view of the Verona Arena

Asolo

(L) The picturesque rooftops of Asolo

Known as la *città dei cento orizzonti* ("the city of the hundred horizons"), the medieval hilltop town of Asolo presides over a tightly grouped range of gentle peaks in the foothills of the Dolomites. From first glance, it's easy to see why the idyllic town has long attracted and inspired artists and writers. At the end of the fifteenth century, Cardinal Bembo, one of the most eminent literary figures of his day, is said to have coined the verb *asolare* to describe the experience of spending one's time in pleasurable aimlessness. The poets Gabriele D'Annunzio and Robert Browning were both inspired by the town's atmosphere and charm; Browning's last published work, *Asolando*, was written here in 1889. With its lofty location and intimate scale, Asolo's arcaded streets, villas and gardens conjure the air of an elegant retreat. An unhurried pace encourages unplanned, lingering afternoons around the town's quiet piazzas and viewpoints over the sweeping Veneto plain.

Friuli-Venezia Giulia

Borders give Friuli-Venezia Giulia its frisson. Trieste looks seaward with Habsburg grandeur, literary cafés and the *bora* wind in its streets, while the Carso turns inland to limestone plateaus, caves and Slovene influences. Aquileia's extraordinary mosaics, Grado's tranquil lagoon and Cividale's Lombard treasures reveal the region's many layers, where Roman and early Christian heritage meets dramatic river gorges, Adriatic island landscapes and a rich, multilingual culture.

Trieste

(T) Trieste's own Grand Canal

Framed by green hills and white limestone cliffs, Trieste offers a distinct atmosphere of grandeur blended with unexpected cosmopolitan twists. While its grand Castello di San Giusto Habsburg fortress, perched atop San Giusto, overlooks remnants of the Roman basilica and forum, and serves glorious views of the bright-blue Adriatic, often swept by the force of the bora wind, back on lower ground, the city's broad squares are adorned with spectacular Neoclassical buildings. Meanwhile, Trieste's much-photographed canal, clustered with open-air literary cafés, is a reminder that, just like Venice and its lagoon, Trieste has enjoyed a glorious seafaring past. Built up by Austria as the Habsburg Empire's great port, it remains Central European in spirit and appearance, with a grand seafront.

Grotta Gigante & THE Carso

A windswept limestone plateau of scrub, caves, villages and hard white rock that extends east into Slovenia's Istrian plateau, the Carso begins almost at Trieste's shoulder. Among the largest show caves in the world, the Carso's most spectacular accessible opening is Grotta Gigante. Enormous in scale, descending into its vast chamber feels akin to witnessing geology transformed into an architectural spectacle, with stalactites and stalagmites dwarfed by the cavern around them. Above ground, the Carso has a stony borderland character that feels far removed from the vineyards and lagoon plains to the west. Walks here reveal sinkholes, views back towards the Adriatic, and settlements shaped by Italian and Slovene presence. Paired together, Grotta Gigante and the Carso reveal Friuli-Venezia Giulia at its most enticingly unearthly.

(O, L, T) In and around the Grotta Gigante

Aquileia

Bordered by the Tagliamento in the west and the Isonzo in the east, the triangle of flatlands west of Trieste and south of Udine present mile after mile of maize fields, tinkling streams, and market gardens. Within this landscape, sits Aquileia. Formerly the Roman capital of Friuli, and a major city of the ancient world, today Aquileia draws the archeologically minded to its atmospheric ruins and basilica, which is best-known for its immense fourth-century floor mosaic. Among the most important monuments of early Christendom, beyond being remarkable for their age, Aquileia's mosaic marvels are also notable for their freshness, with detailed depictions of animals, vines, symbolic scenes and decorative patterns laid out like a secret visual language. Beyond the basilica, the remains of its Roman city reveal Aquileia's status as a threshold between classical Rome and Christian Europe.

(L) Ancient floor mosaic of a deer in the basilica; (T) Ruins of the ancient public square; (B) Basilica di Santa Maria Assunta

Grado & ITS lagoon

South of Aquileia, isolated among lagoons, the ancient island-town of Grado was once the gateway through which Aquileia traded with Syria, Cyprus, Arabia and Asia Minor. Enjoying its heyday under the Austrians who developed it as a health resort due to the presence of curative sand and waters, Grado's historic centre has three early Christian buildings, grouped close together in a cluster of old streets. While Grado is one of the best places in the northern Adriatic for relaxing on the beach, most people come here to explore the Laguna di Grado by boat. Covering around ninety square kilometres, it boasts a myriad of canals and islands that were once inhabited by fishermen. Still dotted with their casoni, traditional houses built with mud and reeds, the lagoon is a place of soft light, gently sloping sandbanks, reeds, birds, tides and wide horizons.

(O) An aerial view of Grado; (L) The area's watery landscape; (T) Sunset from Grado's beach; (B) The lagoon area is ideal for slow exploration

VMPRAESIDIVMCONFVGIMVSSDEIGENITRIX

Cividale del Friuli

Set above the aquamarine Natisone River, Cividale del Friuli preserves a picturesque centre and extraordinary medieval monuments that saw it earn UNESCO World Heritage Centre status. The town's ancient name, Foro Iulii, gave Friuli its name, and its layered past reflects the region's long role as a meeting point for Roman, Lombard, Venetian, Slavic and Central European cultures. Founded in 50 BC by Julius Caesar at the picturesque point where the Natisone River valley opens onto the plain, Cividale del Friuli became the capital of the first Lombard duchy in the sixth century AD. Today, the town's greatest treasure is the eighth-century Tempietto Longobardo, a rare survivor of the Lombard period. With its river gorge, bridges and medieval streets, Cividale del Friuli is hard to beat for travellers who want to experience Friuli-Venezia Giulia distilled into one compact, pretty place.

(L) In Cividale del Friuli's historic centre; (T) Historic bridges connect the old town; (B) Ancient cobbled streets

Emilia-Romagna

Follow the old Via Emilia and this enticing region reveals itself, town by town. Bologna tempts with porticoes, politics, university life and famously rich cooking, while Modena and Parma have also turned food into civic identity without losing sight of their cathedrals, theatres and handsome streets. Eastwards, Ferrara spreads out in Renaissance order, Ravenna glows from within, and San Leo rises sharply on its rock above the gentler countryside below.

Bologna

Capital of Emilia-Romagna, Bologna is also Italy's capital of heartily rich cuisine, and one of the country's best-looking cities to boot. Its compact core is startlingly medieval in plan. An array of red brick buildings with distinctive tiled roofs and balconies radiate from the great central square of Piazza Maggiore. Bologna also boasts some tremendously grand Gothic and Renaissance architecture and, most conspicuously, the Due Torri, the city's own leaning towers. At the centre of Piazza del Nettuno, the Neptune Fountain, created by Giambologna in the late sixteenth century, is one of the most celebrated symbols of the city. In the twentieth century, the city itself became a symbol of socialism, when "Red Bologna" served as the Italian Left's stronghold and spiritual home, a status that evolved from the resistance movement during the German occupation of World War II.

(L) Empty Bologna streets at sunrise

Modena

Declaring itself the "spiritual capital" of Emilia, Modena has a number of verifiable claims to fame. Great motorsports names such as Ferrari, Lamborghini and Maserati are linked to the town, and celebrated at the Modena Terra di Motori every spring. The late Pavarotti was also a native of the city. The area's balsamic vinegar has become a cult product around the world, and Modena's Duomo, a UNESCO World Heritage Site, is one of the finest Romanesque buildings in Italy, with exquisite sculptural decoration lending the stonework narrative weight. Around the cathedral, Modena's labyrinthine centre has the dignified air of an affluent provincial town, with a compact, concentric medieval core bisected by Via Emilia, which runs along the edge of Piazza Grande. This square is the nominal centre of town, where stone buildings and arcades form the focus of much of Modena's everyday life.

(L) Modena's cathedral and bell tower; (T) A Ferrari F1-89 racecar at Museo Casa Enzo Ferrari; (B) Local statue of Perseus

Parma

Another of Italy's great gourmet cities, Parma's name is synonymous with epicurean pleasures, thanks to the surrounding province producing some of the country's most admired ingredients – namely, Parma ham and Parmesan cheese. The city itself has the cultivated air of a wealthy Emilian centre, with refined streets, churches, theatres, and the artistic heritage of Correggio contributing to its cultural weight. The foremost painter of the Parma school of the High Renaissance, Correggio was responsible for some of the powerful works of the sixteenth century, the most famous of which, the *Assumption of the Virgin*, is found in the dome of the Duomo di Parma. A masterwork of Renaissance illusionism, it depicts the Virgin Mary floating up through a sea of limbs, faces and swirling clouds.

(O) Sunshine over Parma's streets; (L) Classical statuary detail; (T) The mouthwatering main attraction in Parma

Ferrara

Shaped by the Este family, an eccentric dynasty that ranked as a major political force throughout the Renaissance, Ferrara is one of Italy's most distinctive towns. While the Este dukes kept the main artists of the day in commissions and created one of the most elegant urban conurbations of the period, at the end of the sixteenth century, with no heir to inherit their lands, the Este were forced to hand over Ferrara to the papacy. After effectively collapsing into a ghost town of empty streets and clogged-up canals, it's since dusted itself down and transformed itself into a vibrant, provincial town of grand squares, restored medieval palaces and portico-lined streets, with the brick walls, towers and moat of Castello Estense giving Ferrara a sense of stately medieval drama.

(L) Castello Estense; (T) Statues of Borso and Niccolò III d'Este on the Palazzo Municipale; (B) A restored palazzo

Ravenna

(T) Basilica di San Vitale

A few kilometres inland from the Adriatic coast, Ravenna is renowned for housing the crowning achievements of Byzantine art, with an impressive eight of its buildings holding UNESCO World Heritage Site status. From the outside, many of its esteemed early-Christian and Byzantine monuments look modest, to the point of almost appearing plain. Inside the Basilica di San Vitale, though, the walls glow with some of the finest mosaics in Europe. Ravenna is also known for its connections to Dante. After being chased out of Florence, he was sheltered here by the ruling Da Polenta family while he finished *The Divine Comedy*, and it was here that he died in 1321. Today, the Museo Dantesco, part of the church of San Francesco complex, contains memorabilia of the poet and his final resting place.

San Leo

Clamped to the summit of a sheer-sided precipice that's been occupied since Roman times, the medieval village of San Leo commands the surrounding Marecchia Valley countryside for almost as far as the eye can see. Certainly one of the most memorable silhouettes in northern Italy, generations have admired the fortress for which San Leo is best known. Besides being praised by Machiavelli, Dante modelled the terrain of his Purgatory on it, while Pietro Bembo described it as Italy's "most beautiful implement of war". Approaching San Leo is an unforgettable experience in itself. The village rises like a natural fortress, with its buildings gathered on the summit and the great stronghold anchoring the rock above. The old village also boasts two churches. The ninth-century Pieve, built by Byzantine-influenced architects from Ravenna, was fashioned from material salvaged from a Roman temple to Jupiter. Just behind it, sunk into the ground, is a sixth-century chapel that was founded by, and later dedicated to, St Leo.

(O) San Leo's fantastical location; (L) A carved detail in the village; (T) Small shops are tucked into the stone structures; (B) Red poppies in bloom in the surrounding countryside

Tuscany

No region carries a heavier burden of expectation than Tuscany, yet the places themselves still have the power to surprise. Florence is dense with Renaissance invention, Siena remains medieval, proud and steep, and Pisa and Lucca showcase different kinds of marble and walled elegance. San Gimignano, Volterra and the Val d'Orcia take the route into hill-town country, before Elba shifts the landscape out to sea.

Florence

Widely celebrated as the most beautiful city in Italy since the early nineteenth century, Florence has no equal in Europe when it comes to Renaissance treasures, with Giotto, Masaccio, Donatello, Botticelli, Leonardo and Michelangelo all intricately woven into the fabric of this handsome city. The pinnacle of Brunelleschi's astonishing cathedral dome dominates the cityscape, and the close-up view is even more breathtaking, thanks to the way the multicoloured Duomo rises beside the marble-clad Baptistry. Down towards the River Arno, Florence's spell continues to swell. Just beyond the broad Piazza della Signoria, site of the towering Palazzo Vecchio, the river is spanned by the medieval Ponte Vecchio, with the exquisite church of San Miniato al Monte glistening on the hill.

(L) Florence's Cathedral Santa Maria del Fiore

Siena

Established as a Roman colony by Augustus, Siena is quick to capture visitor's souls. Immediately enchanting, the city's ancient walls cradle a majestic Gothic ensemble, and its physical and spiritual heart – the scallop-shaped Piazza Il Campo – is arguably Italy's loveliest square. Site of the Siena Palio, Italy's most spectacular festival event (a twice-yearly bareback horse race), Il Campo is also home to Palazzo Pubblico, a magnificent medieval town hall that still serves as a civic office. Siena's most striking expressions of Italian Gothic architecture can be found in the Siena Duomo. Home to famous works like Michelangelo's *Saint Paul* and Bernini's *Mary Magdalene*, the cathedral's marble mosaic floor is among the best of its kind in the world, while its striking black-and-white striped interior, a symbol of the city, creates an illusory hypnotic effect.

(L) Medieval beauty in Siena; (T) Piazza Il Campo; (B) Riders compete in the Palio

Pisa

While Pisa's Leaning Tower (Torre Pendente) serves as a shorthand image for Italy, this is but one component of the breathtaking Campo dei Miracoli (Field of Miracles), where the Duomo, Baptistry and Camposanto (quite possibly the most beautiful cemetery in the world) complete a dazzling architectural ensemble. All date from Pisa's Golden Age, the eleventh to the thirteenth centuries, when the city was one of the Mediterranean's great maritime powers, and their collective impact is one of delicate grace and improbable beauty. Beyond the Campo, along the Arno River, Pisa reveals its illustrious maritime past at the Arsenale Mediceo, a sixteenth-century shipyard housing the Museo delle Navi Antiche di Pisa (Museum of Ancient Ships). Another riverside highlight is the dazzling sky-blue Palazzo Blu, which holds a permanent collection of regional art from the fourteenth to the twentieth centuries.

(O) Pisa's Duomo and Leaning Tower; (L) Reclining in front of the Duomo; (T) The Palazzo Blu

Lucca

(T) Piazza dell'Anfiteatro

Enclosed by a broad, imposing ring of Renaissance walls fronted by gardens that now serve as one of Italy's prettiest promenades, Lucca is the most graceful and polished of Tuscany's provincial capitals. Consistently lovely, and full of life, much of Lucca's centre is free from traffic. While the focus of its compact centro storico is centred on the vast Piazza Napoleone, its social heart is Piazza San Michele, just to the north. Formerly the site of an ancient Roman forum that served as the city's political, religious, and commercial hub for almost 2000 years, today this lively square is fringed with shops and cafés. Beyond, Lucca is speckled with Romanesque churches, quiet lanes, and handsome piazzas, following a street plan that still hints at its Roman origins, with Piazza dell'Anfiteatro preserving the distinct oval outline of the Roman amphitheatre it was built on.

San Gimignano

Built by feuding nobles of the twelfth and thirteenth centuries, the handsome hill-town of San Gimignano evokes the appearance of medieval Tuscany more than any other location, with its skyline of medieval towers soaring over a ridge of stone streets and vineyards giving it an extraordinary drama few places in Italy can match. Beyond the striking silhouette that gave rise to it being known as the "Town of Fine Towers", San Gimignano, a designated UNESCO World Heritage Site, is stacked with glorious public spaces and architecture. Highlights include the twelfth-century Duomo di San Gimignano, which boasts spectacularly vivid frescoes, and the triangular Piazza della Cisterna, lined with medieval residences now housing beautiful gelaterias and cafés. There are few better places to enjoy local Vernaccia di San Gimignano, a crisp white wine produced from ancient grape varieties grown on nearby sandstone hills.

(L) Medieval towers in San Gimignano; (T) The town's romantic skyline atop a hill; (B) Cheese and salami on display

Volterra

Built on a high plateau enclosed by volcanic hills between Siena and the sea, dramatically-sited Volterra prompted D.H. Lawrence to write that "it gets all the wind and sees all the world – a sort of inland island". Chiming with that, seashells can often be seen embedded in the paving of streets and squares. Though busy, Volterra retains a soft-edged atmosphere, with its walled medieval core made from Tuscan yellow-grey panchino stone. Formerly home to one of the most ancient Etruscan communities, Volterra still abounds in Etruscan artefacts, as revealed in the Museo Etrusco Guarnacci. Specialising in the region's rich Etruscan history, and holding some truly remarkable treasures, this ranks among Italy's most important archaeological museums. West of the pretty Parco Archeologico, there's an Etruscan acropolis, while the other side of town boasts a Teatro Romano and other Roman-era buildings.

(L) Washing adorns tiled buildings; (T) Atmospheric alfresco dining; (B) In Museo Etrusco Guarnacci

Val d'Orcia, Pienza & Montalcino

Running south of Siena towards Mount Amiata in southern Tuscany, the Val d'Orcia is a UNESCO-designated agricultural and cultural valley that almost seems too bucolically perfect to be true. Presenting its dreamily painterly self as a scene of rolling hills, cypress-lined roads, and medieval villages, the valley is the heartland for many world-renowned Italian wines, pecorino cheese, and extra-virgin olive oil, with the tiny, perfectly preserved village of Pienza adding a glorious touch of Renaissance magic. Pienza was established as a Utopian "New Town" by a local boy made good, Enea Silvio Bartolomeo Piccolomini, when he became Pope Pius II in 1458. Meanwhile, Montalcino adds a more robust note, thanks to its fortress, circuit of walls, and steep streets. Quiet and unassumingly affluent, Montalcino is best known for its high-quality Brunello di Montalcino, a red DOCG wine, Italy's highest tier of wine classification.

(O) A lush Tuscan landscape; (L) An ancient archway frames the Val d'Orcia landscape; (T) Narrow Montalcino streets; (B) Ripe grapes in a Montalcino vineyard

Elba

(T) Portoferraio

Part of the Tuscan Archipelago, a chain of seven principal islands sprinkled between the Ligurian and Tyrrhenian seas off Italy's west coast, Elba is an idyllic place with exceptionally clear water, fine white-sand beaches, and a lush, sloping, wooded interior. At almost 30km long and 20km wide, Elba is Italy's third-largest island after Sicily and Sardinia, and has plenty to keep most types of travellers happy. While families come for the beach resorts, hikers and serenity seekers head inland to enjoy the peaceful walks on the wilder side, while coastal towns like Portoferraio present Elba's maritime legacies (most people know the island as Napoleon's place of exile) and cosmopolitan history. The Romans described Elba as "the island of good wines", a reputation Elban wines retain to this day. After the Roman era, control of the island passed from Pisa to Genoa, then to the Medici, Spain, Turkey and finally France, and this mix has left its mark on all aspects of latter-day life on Elba.

Umbria

Without a coast or a single dominant city, Umbria draws attention in quieter ways. Golden Perugia gives the region weight and urban energy, Assisi brings pilgrimage and frescoed devotion, and Gubbio, Spoleto and Orvieto rise in stone from hills and cliffs. Then the Piano Grande breaks the pattern entirely: a high, open plain beneath the Sibillini, rich in shifting weather, flowers, pasture and sky.

Perugia

(T) The ancient medieval aqueduct, Perugia

Provincial capital of Umbria, Perugia mixes the convenience of big-city amenities with Etruscan intrigue, medieval towers, grand Gothic palazzi, Renaissance art, and modern-day student energy from a hilltop that overlooks the Tiber River valley. The town hinges around a single street, Corso Vannucci, named after the city's most celebrated artist, Pietro Vannucci. Lined with bustling pavement cafés, this is one of Italy's greatest people-watching streets. A sense of drama derives from the steep lanes that climb towards Perugia's old centre, where dark stone buildings and enclosed streets give the city a more serious mood than many Umbrian towns, which tend to have softer edges. At its heart, Piazza IV Novembre gathers the cathedral, Palazzo dei Priori and Fontana Maggiore into one of central Italy's great civic spaces.

Assisi

Inseparable from St Francis and the spiritual reputation that made Umbria known as the land of saints, Assisi is one of Italy's great places of pilgrimage. Climbing the slopes of Monte Subasio in pale stone terraces, Assisi's supreme monument is the Basilica di San Francesco. Built to house the saint's remains, and decorated with some of the most important frescos in Italy, including Giotto's dazzling depiction of the life of St Francis, this also houses one of the most overwhelming collections of art outside a gallery anywhere in the world. Started in 1228, two years after the saint's death, it was financed by donations that flooded in from all over Europe. Beyond the basilica, Assisi's main square, Piazza del Comune, is dominated by the Tempio di Minerva, an enticing and perfectly-preserved classical facade from the first century.

(L, T) The Basilica of St Francis of Assisi; (B) The grand nave with stained glass, starry vaults and Giotto frescoes in the basilica

Gubbio

The most medieval of Umbrian towns, Gubbio is instantly likeable, with picture-book-pretty pink-stone houses capped by orange-tiled roofs. And all this in a setting that's just as gorgeous, thanks to the forest-clad mountains of the Apennines rearing up behind. A broad and largely unspoilt plain stretches out in front of the town, and the whole ensemble, especially on grey, windswept days, maintains Gubbio's mountain-outpost atmosphere. Palaces and churches seem to grow directly from the hillside, rising towards the fourteenth-century, fortress-like Palazzo dei Consoli. Almost unique to the town, Gubbio's Porte della Morte ("doors of death") add an extra layer of intrigue. Narrow, bricked-up doorways can be seen wedged into the facades of its medieval townhouses; the story goes that these were used to carry a coffin out of a house. Then, having been tainted with death, they were sealed up out of superstitious fear.

(O) Gubbio's Roman theatre; (L) Narrow Gubbio streets;
(T) View from the archways; (B) Modern lights in a medieval town

Spoleto

Divided into the medieval, hilltop Upper Town, which is home to the Duomo and most key museums and galleries, and the predominantly modern Lower Town, Spoleto is among Umbria's most charming large towns. Poised between cultivated hill-town elegance and the wilder country of the Valnerina, Spoleto's old centre rises steeply through lanes, piazzas and stone houses towards the Rocca Albornoziana. Located to the east of town, this fortress of towers, crenellations and sheer walls embodies most people's notion of what a classic castle should look like. Arguably the best thing to do in Spoleto is to walk out to the Ponte delle Torri, the town's favoured postcard image, and an astonishing example of medieval engineering. Within a minute of leaving Piazza Campello's shady gardens, walkers are served superb views over countryside, along with a dramatic panorama across the Tessino gorge and south to the mountains of Castelmonte.

(L) Spoleto's Duomo

Piano Grande

One of central Italy's most extraordinary landscapes, the eerie, expansive Piano Grande stretches, uninterrupted by tree, hedge or habitation, for kilometres and kilometres. Lying beneath the Sibillini Mountains, and ringed by bare, whaleback mountains, it's part of the Parco Nazionale dei Monti Sibillini, where high mountain scenery forms the region's wilder eastern edge. Astonishingly open by Umbrian standards, in spring and early summer, wildflowers spread waves of colour across the plateau. In other seasons, it feels stark and windswept. Around the year, the Piano Grande provides a powerful elemental contrast with Umbria's walled hill-towns and wooded valleys. All but unknown a decade or so ago, the isolated village of Castelluccio hangs above it, and although no longer the sole preserve of shepherds, the village remains a relatively quiet and unspoilt base, and the ideal starting point for countless country walks.

(L) Castelluccio, surrounded by flowers and mountains; (T) Shepherd and his flock; (B) View over the plateau

Orvieto

Located out on a limb from the rest of Umbria, Orvieto strikes an unforgettable first impression. Crowning a plug of volcanic lava, the clifftop town rises sheer from the valley floor. In its compact, ancient centre, Orvieto presents one of the greatest Gothic buildings in Italy, its Duomo, a building so beautiful that Pope Leo XIII called it "the Golden Lily of Italian cathedrals", adding that on the Day of Judgement it would float up to heaven carried by its own beauty. The Duomo's façade is a blaze of sculpture, mosaic and striped stone, while inside the Cappella di San Brizio holds Luca Signorelli's fresco cycle, an influential evocation of judgement, resurrection and apocalypse. Orvieto also carries an Etruscan inheritance (it was one of the twelve-strong federation of Etruscan cities), and its subterranean caves showcase Etruscan and medieval antiquities, and the remains of an entire medieval mill.

(O) Orvieto, perched on a sheer cliff; (L) Sixteenth-century St Patrick's Well; (T) Adornment on the Duomo

Le Marche

Le Marche stretches between the Apennines and the Adriatic, often overlooked – and all the better for it. Urbino preserves the elegance of a Renaissance court in pale brick, Frasassi opens a vast world beneath the earth, and the Conero Riviera boasts dramatic cliffs and crystalline water. Loreto draws pilgrims from across the Catholic world, while Ascoli Piceno captivates with its honey-coloured travertine piazzas and quietly confident sense of place.

Urbino

Birthplace of Raphael, and master-planned to be the "Ideal City of the Renaissance, Urbino is a handsome hilltop town built from pale bricks and intellectual ambition. Its golden age came under Federico da Montefeltro, a visionary soldier-duke who transformed a remote court into one of Europe's most significant cultural centres. Walled and austere, today Urbino is a jumble of Renaissance and medieval houses, churches and palazzi. Its historic centre, dominated by a stellar attraction, the Palazzo Ducale, is a UNESCO World Heritage Site. Designed to embody order, proportion, and intellectual ambition, Federico da Montefeltro employed some of the greatest artists and architects of the time to construct and decorate the palazzo. The result is a remarkable building that's at once elegant, restrained, and emblematic of the Ideal City Montefeltro envisaged and realised, perhaps improbably, given Urbino's original remoteness and somewhat humble courtly standing.

(L) Urbino's Palazzo Ducale

Grotte di Frasassi

Located in the green heart of Le Marche, a region celebrated for its historic opera houses, the Grotte di Frasassi offer a very different kind of theatre: one of subterranean drama. Part of the Gola della Rossa and Frasassi Regional Natural Park, and among Europe's most spectacular karst complexes, the caves were carved over 1.4 million years by a slow but relentless geological process. As rainwater seeped through fissures in the limestone, sulphur-rich waters associated with the nearby Sentino River gradually dissolved the rock, hollowing out immense, cathedral-like chambers. The largest of these was discovered only in 1971, and visitors can now explore just over a kilometre of its vast caverns and tunnels. Among the most remarkable formations are the petrified "Niagara Falls", a giant's head with a strikingly Roman profile, a chamber whose stalagmites resemble candles with their holders, and a formation that resembles the pipes of a grand organ.

(O, L) In the Grotte di Frasassi; (T) The grotto's exterior;
(B) Valadier Temple at the cave's entrance

Conero Riviera

With its white cliffs, blanched pebble beaches, thick forests and easy-going resorts, the Conero Riviera is the northern Adriatic's most spectacular and pleasurable stretch of coastline. Providing a dramatic contrast from the long, flat ribbon of Adriatic resorts that dominate much of the shoreline around these parts, here, south of Ancona, white limestone cliffs plunge into turquoise water, with the wooded slopes of Monte Conero rising behind, and slipping into the sea from an altitude of 572m. The most stunning stretch of coast, a series of tiny coves at the base of Monte Conero between the seaside villages of Portonovo and Sirolo, is most rewardingly explored by boat. Both villages are beautiful bases, with Portonovo's Hotel Fortino Napoleonico located in a former Napoleonic fort, and Sirolo serving extraordinary views from its main square, Piazza Veneto, which is located right on the edge of the cliff.

(L) Numana beach on the Conero Riviera; (T) Relaxing in the surf; (B) Portonovo's church

Loreto

(T) The Basilica della Santa Casa is a shrine of Marian pilgrimage in Loreto

One of Italy's major pilgrimage towns, Loreto is visited each year by over four million believers because of one of the Catholic Church's more surreal legends. The story goes that in 1292, when Muslims pushed the Crusaders from Palestine, a band of angels flew the house of Mary, the Santa Casa, from Nazareth to Dalmatia. A few years later, they whisked it across the Adriatic to Loreto. To combat scepticism about this outlandish story, the Vatican later claimed that the Holy House was transported to Loreto aboard a Crusader ship. Either way, Loreta's Santa Casa, housed in a basilica, inspires tremendous religious fervour among pilgrims. While the basilica is grand, and features works by Renaissance luminaries like Bramante, Sansovino, Lotto and Luca Signorelli, the Santa Casa itself is somewhat more modest, with pride of place within the house given to a copy of the famous Black Madonna of Loreto.

CAFFE'
MELETTI

Ascoli Piceno

Located between Monti Sibillini and the Adriatic, Ascoli Piceno is Le Marche's greatest unsung treasure, and lies well off the tourist trail, which is hard to fathom, given its grand architecture, and café-lined central square that's among the most striking in the region. Constructed from pale travertine, Ascoli Piceno's pretty streets and piazzas have a luminous, almost silvery quality, with Piazza del Popolo its dazzling showpiece, quite literally, for its paved floor gleams like water. Hemmed by grand facades, this Renaissance charmer is dominated by the Palazzo dei Capitani. Beyond the square, Ascoli Piceno has a small number of Roman remains, with its churches and museums scattered throughout the old centre. Lively and sociable, the town hosts Le Marche's most flamboyant carnival, and also loves its food, with *olive all'ascolana* (deep-fried breadcrumb-crusted olives stuffed with veal) a local favourite.

(O) Overview of Palazzo dei Capitani; (L) Loggias in Palazzo Vecchio; (T) Medieval stone arches in the town centre

Abruzzo & Molise

Mountains set the tone in Abruzzo and Molise. Gran Sasso and Corno Grande showcase soaring crags, high plateaus and the grandeur of the Apennines, while the national park shelters forests, traditional villages and the possibility of spotting bears, wolves and chamois. Sulmona and Scanno preserve mountain traditions beneath the peaks, and in Molise, Saepinum lies quietly among the fields, its Roman stone long since absorbed into the quiet surrounding pasture and hills.

Gran Sasso & Corno Grande

Showcasing Abruzzo at its most immense, and Italy in one of its most unexpectedly wild guises, Gran Sasso lives up to its name, which means "Great Rock of Italy". An enormous limestone and dolomite mountain massif, Gran Sasso is the centrepiece of the expansive Gran Sasso e Monti della Laga National Park, which protects a richness of wildlife, including wolves, boars, chamois, bears and huge numbers of birds. Rising from Gran Sasso, Corno Grande, the highest peak in the Apennines, is a landmark for hikers and climbers who are drawn to terrain that feels far removed from Italy's crowded art cities and beach resorts. Beneath Como Grande, Calderone Glacier is the sole remaining glacier in Southern Europe, accessed by hikers via the Carlo Franchetti mountain lodge (Rifugio Franchetti).

(L) Gran Sasso's summit

Sulmona

Flanked by bleak mountains southeast of L'Aquila, and bristling with legends about its most famous son, Ovid, Sulmona is an affluent provincial settlement that owes its wealth to gold jewellery and sugared almonds *(confetti)*. Overshadowed by the mountainous bulk of the Majella, with a dark tangle of a historical centre lined with imposing palaces, Sulmona is surprisingly under-visited. Corso Ovidio, the main street, cuts through the centre and leads up to Piazza XX Settembre, passing the Gothic-Renaissance Annunziata palazzo, where Ovid is depicted on an intriguing statue, and Piazza del Carmine, which hosts the hefty Romanesque portal of San Francesco della Scarpa, and an impressive Gothic aqueduct that was built to supply water to the town and power to its wool mills.

(L) One of the medieval gateways into Sulmona; (T) Sulmona's historic town centre; (B) Intricate cathedral tympanum

Scanno

(T) Scanno

Reached by passing through the spectacular Gole del Sagittario, with hairpin bends widening out at the glassy green Lago di Scanno, Scanno is one of Abruzzo's most memorable mountain towns. A well-preserved medieval village encircled by mountains, Scanno's narrow streets, stone houses and steep setting give it a powerful old-world atmosphere. In 1951, Henri Cartier-Bresson photographed the village, largely focusing on the traditional dress worn by Scanno's women, and that sense of tradition is still in evidence today, with some of the town's more elderly residents often seen wearing long, dark, pleated skirts and bodices with a patterned apron that suggests a possible origin in Asia Minor. Also known for wool production and lace-making, Scanno's pleasure is wandering the old town, soaking up its sense of community and cultural continuity with centuries-old traditions.

Parco Nazionale d'Abruzzo

At four hundred square kilometres, the Parco Nazionale d'Abruzzo is Italy's third-largest national park. A protected mountain landscape of forests, valleys, villages and high country, here the Apennines feel alive. Offering excellent hiking, the park also contains around one hundred indigenous species. Among the park's most important animals are the Apennine wolf and the Marsican brown bear. Until recently, an endangered species, the park now hosts thirty to fifty bears, but, as with the wolves, the closest most visitors get to encountering them in the wild is by spotting footprints in mud or snow. To see both up close, there's a bear reserve near the visitor centre, and wolves can be seen in the dedicated Museo del Lupo Appenninico in Civitella Alfadena. Meanwhile, across the park's expanse, trails lead through beech woods, meadows and ridge country speckled with serene stone-built villages.

(O) Autumn foliage and waterfall in the national park; (L) A red stag; (T) Hiking in the park

Saepinum

Surrounded by a lush, open plain and fringed by the foothills of the Matese mountains, the ruins of Saepinum present Italy's finest example of a provincial Roman town. Somewhat ironically, the main reason Saepinum has such an important status today is that it was never important. Aside from being sacked by the Saracens in the ninth century, the town has seen little action. Over the centuries, its inhabitants added only a handful of farms and cottages and eventually moved south to the hilltop site of present-day Sepino, though a few farms and cottages lie on Saepinum's peripheries, and the sight of grazing sheep and chickens lends the site a unique quality. Sometimes referred to as a "hidden Pompeii", Saepinum contains many well-preserved buildings, including a forum, senate house, temple, baths, and marketplace, with a small museum presenting artefacts and artwork recovered during excavations.

(L) Saepinum from above; (T) Anicent pillars; (B) A triumphal arch

Campania

Campania wastes no time in declaring itself. Naples is dense, loud and ancient, its historic centre alive above and below ground, while Pompeii and Herculaneum preserve a vivid snapshot of Roman life beneath Vesuvius. Across the bay, Capri and Ischia emerge from volcanic waters. To the south, the Amalfi Coast clings to dramatic cliffs, while Paestum's Greek temples stand in bright Mediterranean light beyond Salerno.

Naples centro storico

(T) The sweep of Naples bay, with Vesuvius in the distance

Like its Mount Vesuvius backdrop, Naples is a firecracker of a city. From the depths of its subterranean caves, to its erotic ancient art, Naples smoulders with rough-round-the-edges appeal, and unexpected treasures. Large, loud, sprawling, and energetic, the area between Piazza Garibaldi and Via Toledo, roughly corresponding to the old Roman Neapolis (much of which is still unexcavated beneath the ground), makes up the centro storico, with its main streets still following the paths of old Roman roads. This is by far the liveliest part of town: dense, noisy and expressive, with churches, shrines, palazzi, workshops, food stalls and apartment balconies pressed into a maze of narrow, dark lanes. Unlike Italy's more curated historic centres, Naples' centro storico feels inhabited, unpolished, and turned up to full volume.

Pompeii

Once a sophisticated Roman trading town populated by moneyed patricians, Pompeii was buried beneath metres of ash in the devastating eruption of Mount Vesuvius in 79 AD, and today offers unparalleled insights into the lives of Roman citizens during the imperial era. One of Pompeii's most powerful aspects is how intimate everyday life feels tangible through its well-preserved bakeries, bars, bathhouses, courtyards and streets worn smooth by the feet of its citizens, while the grand houses, theatres and brothels broaden the site's social scope. Highlights include the Forum, the luxurious villas of Via di Mercurio, and its epic amphitheatre, one of the oldest and most intact in Italy. Grandest of all is the restored Villa dei Misteri (Villa of the Mysteries). The best-preserved of all Pompeii's palatial houses, it derives its name from a series of paintings depicting the initiation of a young woman into the Dionysiac Mysteries.

(O, L, T) The famous excavated site of Pompeii

Herculaneum

The ash-buried city of Herculaneum might be smaller than its sister city of Pompeii, but it's less crowded, and many of its ruins are even better preserved. The pyroclastic material that covered Herculaneum carbonized, preserving organic materials like food, paper and wood. In its heyday, Herculaneum was a residential town, which meant there was no central open space or forum, just streets of villas and shops, cut, as usual, by two straight main thoroughfares that crossed in the centre. Also notable is that many buildings were preserved to a remarkable height; their upper storeys, wooden fittings, vivid wall paintings and domestic spaces evoke a startling sense of immediacy. This, along with the presence of hundreds of petrified humans, gives Herculaneum a distinctly haunting atmosphere.

(L) Wall mosaic of Neptune and Amphitrite in Herculaneum; (T) Casa del Rilievo di Telefo; (B) Excavated ruins

Capri

Imperial, artistic, aristocratic and cinematic, Capri has been pursued, possessed and mythologized for two thousand years. Jutting from the sea off the far end of the Sorrentine peninsula, the island has also long been esteemed as the most romantic area of the Bay of Naples. In fact, Capri, home of the mythological Sirens, was the private love island of Roman emperors. Rising from deep-blue water in the form of cliffs, terraces and whitewashed lanes, with dramatic vistas materialising around every bend, Capri's romantic allures live on today in its beautiful beaches, lush interior landscape and splendid architecture. Nestled between two mountains, Capri Town is centred on Piazza Umberto I. Better known as "La Piazzetta", behind it lies a maze of charming streets, and steps that lead to a domed seventeenth-century church, Santo Stefano. Elsewhere, there are elegant villas to explore, with the Arco Naturale and Grotta di Matermania on hand for natural beauty.

(L) Bright blue seas from Monte Solaro on Capri

Ischia

Rising from the sea as a series of pointy green hummocks, Ischia is the Bay of Naples' great volcanic garden, and its biggest island. Towering over the island, Monte Epomeo is Ischia's highest peak: a rugged, dormant volcano that's thick with a forest so lush, visitors might be forgiven for thinking they're in the tropics. Shaped by thermal springs, beaches, small villages and slopes, Ischia's most arresting sight is the Castello Aragonese, a fortress perched on a craggy islet that's linked to the main island by a causeway. Seen from the water or the shore, it gives the island a medieval drama that counters its softer, lusher aspects. Vineyards, and a busy harbour town add texture, with La Mortella, an exotic garden created by the British composer William Walton and his wife Susana, adding elegance. Fertile and restorative, above all else, Ischia feels vital and authentically Campanian.

(O) Ponte Aragonese Chiesa dell Immacolata;
(L) Fountains and pathways in the hot springs on Ischia;
(T) Narrow village alleys; (B) A boat moored up in the harbour

Amalfi Coast

Spanning the southern side of Sorrento's peninsula, the Amalfi Coast is justifiably often touted as being Europe's most beautiful stretch of coast. South of the Bay of Naples, the coastal road clings to cliffs above a staggeringly beautiful stretch of sea, passing coves, terraces, lemon groves, tiny beaches and towns, all squeezed between mountain and water. While Positano provides towering vertical glamour, its houses tumbling in tiers towards the shore, Amalfi, cradled in a wide cleft in the cliffs, has a crumbly attractiveness to its whitewashed courtyards and alleys, and a spirit that harks back to its days as an Edwardian seaside resort. A wonderful way for walkers to explore the coast is via the well-marked Path of the Gods (Il Sentiero degli Dei), a 6km trail that undulates along ridges beside terraced slopes and sheer karst walls.

(L) The quintessential view of Positano; (T) The Amalfi Coast's vertiginous cliffs and karsts; (B) Colourful ceramics for sale

Paestum

(T) Paestum's Temple of Athena

Spread across a large area at the end of the Piana del Sele, a flat plain grazed by buffalo that produce a good quantity of southern Italy's mozzarella cheese, the ancient site of Paestum is one of the finest places in Europe to encounter the Greek world outside Greece itself. Founded by Greeks from Sybaris in the sixth century BC, and later colonized by the Romans, Paestum's significance stems from the three great, golden-stoned Doric temples that rise from the ruins of the ancient settlement. Astonishingly complete, in the right light, the columns almost seem to glow, and their scale is staggering. Of the site's three temples, which are among the best-preserved of their kind in Europe, the Temple of Neptune, dating from about 450 BC, is the most intact; only its roof and parts of the inner walls are missing. Beyond, the surrounding site is spacious, open, and dotted with intriguing traces of streets, houses and civic buildings.

Puglia

Long, low and sun-baked, Puglia feels unlike anywhere else in Italy. Bari Vecchia is a captivating knot of narrow lanes and hidden shrines, while the enigmatic Castel del Monte rises in splendid isolation. To the north, the Gargano Peninsula and the Tremiti Islands offer ancient forests, cliffs and crystalline waters. Further south, the conical *trulli* of Alberobello dot the countryside, while Lecce glows with Baroque churches and palazzi carved from the region's distinctive limestone.

Bari Vecchia

Bari Vecchia (Old Bari) boasts one of southern Italy's most intriguing old quarters: a tight maze of lanes packed onto the promontory between the city's two harbours. The commercial and administrative capital of Puglia, a university town, and southern Italy's second city, Bari, was already a thriving centre when the Romans arrived, and later served as the seat of the Byzantine governor of southern Italy. Later, under the Normans, the city rivalled Venice as a maritime centre and – following the seizure of the remains of St Nicholas – as a place of pilgrimage. Later still, Mussolini instituted a university and left a legacy of Fascist-era architecture. Hardly a typical tourist destination, Bari's old town is an attractive labyrinth of seemingly endless passages that weave through courtyards and under arches, with its Basilica di San Nicola providing a grand spiritual anchor that draws pilgrims to the relics of St Nicholas.

(L) Bari Vecchia at sunrise

Castel del Monte

A lone presence atop a low hill, Castel del Monte's isolation intensifies its mystery. As the countryside opens, the castle rises, and the building's uncanny perfection dominates the horizon. Built for Frederick II in the thirteenth century, this is the most extraordinary of all Puglia's castles, and one of the finest surviving examples of Swabian architecture. An octagonal castle, with eight towers, clean geometry and a severe beauty, a mystery surrounds its intended purpose. Although there was once an iron gate that could be lowered over the main entrance, there are no other visible signs of fortification, and the castle may have served as a hunting lodge. That said, the mathematical precision involved in its construction, and the preoccupation with the number eight, has intrigued writers for centuries, with some arguing that it's an enormous astrological calendar, or that Frederick may have had the octagonal Omar mosque in Jerusalem in mind when he designed it.

(L) Castel del Monte; (T) The castle from above; (B) In the stark interior of one of its turrets

Gargano & Vieste

A hilly, forested promontory thrust into the Adriatic, the Gargano rises like an island above the long wheatfields of the Tavoliere. It has a remarkably diverse landscape. Beaches and lagoons lie to the north, with a rocky, indented eastern coast, and a mountainous, green heartland of oak and beech trees that's more reminiscent of a Germanic forest than a corner of southern Italy. Though extremely isolated for centuries, visited only by pilgrims making their way along the valley to Monte Sant'Angelo and its shrine, these days it draws increasing numbers of visitors, especially around the seaside resort of Vieste, though the establishment of a national park protects it from overbearing development. Jutting into the Adriatic on two promontories, Vieste has some excellent beaches, and an interesting historic core, with its old town scenically sited on the easternmost of the two promontories.

(O) Vieste's harbour; (L) Sailing near the natural arch of San Felice; (T) On the forrested Puglian islets

Tremiti Islands

(T) Tremiti islands of San Domino and Cretaccio

A tiny cluster of rugged islands off the Gargano coast, the Tremiti Islands are almost entirely given over to tourism in summer, but despite this influx, they remain relatively unspoilt, and the sea is crystal clear. Traditionally a place of exile and punishment, the island in the eleventh century became a site of monastic settlement, and monks from Montecassino on the mainland set about building a fortress-abbey on one of the islands that managed to withstand frequent assaults by the Turks. These days, the Tremiti Islands satisfy visitors' cravings for a calmer pace of life by offering gentle sea crossings, boat trips to sea caves, and walks along pine-scented paths. While San Domino is the greenest and most immediately beautiful island, rocky San Nicola carries more historical weight, with a monastic fortress to wander, and the tiny church of Santa Maria a Mare, built by eleventh-century monks on the site of a ninth-century hermitage, perched spectacularly over the Adriatic.

Alberobello & *trulli* country

Cylindrical, whitewashed buildings with grey conical roofs that taper to a point or sphere, the curious-looking *trulli* can be found dotted throughout the Murge area of Puglia. Often adorned with painted symbols, and unique to the area, although their origins are obscure, it's most likely connected to feudal lords forcing people working their land to build their houses without mortar. That way, the buildings could easily be pulled down if tax inspectors turned up. Though practical in their role as rural storehouses and dwellings, the dense concentration of over 1,500 *trulli* in Alberobello, a UNESCO World Heritage Site, makes the town feel like a fairytale come to life. Most *trulli* are located south of Largo Martellotta in the Rione Monti zone, with the rest to the north in Rione Aia Piccola – and many now serve as enchanting holiday rentals.

(O, L, T, B) Renovated trulli houses in Alberobelllo

Lecce

Majestically Baroque and dubbed the "Florence of the South", Lecce is warmer, softer and more ornate than its northern sister. With a wealth of fine architecture scattered about an appealing old town, as well as a clutch of Roman remains, Lecce's exuberant building styles are the legacy of religious orders (Jesuits, the Teatini and Franciscans) who came to the region at the end of the sixteenth century, bringing an influx of wealth which paid for the opulent churches and palazzi that define the city today. The flowery style of "Leccese Baroque" owed as much to the materials to hand as to the skills of the architects. The soft local sandstone could be intricately carved before hardening with age. Lecce's top attractions include the Basilica di Santa Croce and Piazza Sant'Oronzo, the hub of the old town, named after the first-century bishop of Lecce who went to the lions under Nero.

(L) Opulent baroque carving on Lecce's churches; (T) Sunset over Lecce; (B) Carved details on the Basilica di San Croce

Basilicata & Calabria

In Basilicata and Calabria, the south becomes starker, more mountainous and more startling. Matera's Sassi cut into the rock above a ravine, and nearby cave churches preserve frescoes in shadowed interiors. Elsewhere, Maratea turns to the Tyrrhenian with cliffs and coves. Calabria brings the dazzling water of Tropea and Capo Vaticano, and Reggio faces Sicily across the strait with Greek bronzes and sea wind.

Cripta del Peccato Originale

South of Matera, the Cripta del Peccato Originale (Crypt of the Original Sin) is lauded as the "Sistine Chapel of cave churches". A rock-hewn church in the contrada of Petrapenta, this was the site of a Benedictine rock monastery from the Lombard period. Its fame rests on a cycle of late eighth-century frescoes painted by an artist known as the "Painter of the Flowers of Matera". Depicting surprisingly dynamic scenes, the left wall presents the Apostles, Virgin Queen, and Archangels, with its white background embellished with tendrils of red flowers, while the wall at the back illustrates the creation and moment of original sin. Across the crypt, the painted figures almost seem to emerge from the stone, their colours and lines having survived in a landscape that's seen believers take shelter in caves, ravines and remote monastic settlements across several centuries.

(L) Stunning frescoes in the crypt

Matera

Dating from the Middle Ages when Byzantine and Benedictine monks built rock-hewn churches and monasteries into what are now called the Sassi, Matera is one of Italy's most astonishing townscapes. An intricate series of terraced cave dwellings gouged from the rock and hollowed into the sides of a ravine at the eastern end of Basilicata, the Sassi, literally "stones", were inhabited until the 1950s, when their impoverished residents were forcibly removed and rehoused. Today this national scandal is hard to believe, for the Sassi have been transformed into enchantingly rustic homes, churches, hotels and cultural spaces, with a thirteenth-century Duomo presiding over the site. Aside from being blown away by the marvel of this unique fusion of geology, spirituality and human settlement, visitors today can get a glimpse of life as a former Sassi dweller in the reconstructed Casa Grotta.

(O) Matera clings to a rocky outcrop; (L) The modern scupture, "Terra Mater, Earth and Heaven" in front of Matera's cathedral; (T) In Matera's old town

Maratea

The short stretch of Basilicata's Tyrrhenian coast is the most visually ravishing part of the entire region. A place that sees tall, sheer cliffs rise dramatically above rocky coves and cascade down to sublime beaches, the encircling mountains have kept development to a minimum, which makes Maratea Basilicata's most seductive coastal escape. The town itself has an historic centre of lanes, churches and quiet squares, while the coast below is broken by beaches, coves, and a busy marina, with the wider settlement covering 20km of the coastline, including the hamlets of Castrocucco, Marina, Porto, Fiumicello, Cersuta and Acquafredda. Well-endowed with sandy beaches, including especially fine examples at Fiumicello and Acquafredda, the coast is home to fifty or so grottoes, most accessible only by boat. Beyond the coast, Monte San Biagio (624m) is on hand for rewarding scenic hikes up to the highest point above Maratea.

(L) Colourful shops in Maratea; (T) Marina di Maratea Beach at sunset; (B) A giant sculpture of Cristo Redentore in Maratea

Tropea & Capo Vaticano

Set along a stretch of pale cliffs, turquoise water, and sandy beaches backed by hills, Tropea might just be the prettiest town on the southern Tyrrhenian coast. Built on the edge of steep cliffs, it's also somewhat fashionable, with stacks of seaside charm streaming from its squares and chic cafés. Below town, numerous lovely beaches are within easy walking distance. Tropea's old centre has plenty of character, too, not least the pretty Norman cathedral at the bottom of Via Roma. The views from the upper town over the sea and the church of Santa Maria dell'Isola below are superb. South along the coast, Capo Vaticano brings a wilder note, with headlands, coves, and incredibly clear water. Capo Vaticano also takes in some of the area's most popular beaches, including Grotticelle and Tonicello, which are both spacious enough to handle the heaviest high-season crowds.

(O) Sanctuary of Santa Maria dell'Isola in Tropea; (L) Grotticelle beach; (T) Sunset terrace dining; (B) Red chillies and onions for sale

Reggio Calabria

Standing at the toe of Italy, facing Sicily across the Strait of Messina, Reggio Calabria was one of the first ancient Greek settlements on the Italian mainland, and its greatest treasure is the Bronzi di Riace, two extraordinary fifth-century BC Greek bronzes. Life-sized and technically astonishing, these are among the finest surviving examples of ancient Greek sculpture found anywhere in the world. After being pulled from the sea, they're now displayed in the fascinating Museo Archeologico Nazionale. Beyond the museum, Reggio Calabria's seafront offers one of southern Italy's great promenades, with views across the strait towards Mount Etna on clear days, and the tantalising sense that Sicily is almost within touching distance. At the southern end of the pedestrianized Corso Garibaldi, the remains of sixth-century BC city walls and a Roman bathing complex add another level of historic intrigue.

(L) One of the Riace Bronzes; (T) Monument on the promenade; (B) A drive with a view

Sicily

Sicily has always absorbed arrivals and transformed them. Palermo is noisy, layered and magnificent, Cefalù combines a sandy beach with Norman stone, and the Aeolian Islands see active and dormant volcanoes scattered across the sea. Etna dominates the east with ash, vineyards and black lava, while Taormina, Siracusa, the Val di Noto and Agrigento bring together Greek theatres, Baroque facades and temples on a grand Mediterranean scale.

Palermo

Fast and brash, Palermo is Sicily at its most intense. Shaped by conquest and trade, the island's often chaotic capital is a place that sees Arabic cupolas float above exuberant Baroque facades, high-fashion shops compete with street markets, and walls of graffitied municipal buildings rub shoulders with the crumbling shells of collapsing palazzi. Containing Sicily's greatest concentration of sights, and boasting the biggest historic centre in Italy bar Rome, Palermo is a complex, multifaceted city, with streets that carry the imprint of many cultures: Greek, Arab, Norman, Spanish and Bourbon. Historic Palermo is centred around the Quattro Canti, a gleaming Baroque crossroads that divides it into quadrants. Occupying the southwest quadrant, the maze of tiny streets and tall leaning buildings that make up the Albergheria district has barely changed in several hundred years. With its markets and varied architectural styles, few places conjure the city's multi-layered, multi-cultural character so vividly.

(L) The classic narrow Palermo street scene, with the church of San Matteo at the end

Cefalù

Tucked onto every available centimetre of land beneath a castle-topped crag, Cefalù is nevertheless one of Sicily's busiest international beach resorts. It also leads a double life as a small-scale fishing port, and is home to a mighty cathedral, founded in 1131, which adds an extra point of cultural interest. Taken as a whole, Cefalù somehow manages to strike an unusually harmonious and satisfying balance between beach life, local life, and monumental history. While the Duomo certainly dominates the skyline – with its great twin towers rearing above the flat roofs of the medieval quarter and over a pleasant town that has a tangibly Arabic grid of streets – Cefalù's long sandy beach is arguably its major attraction. Or perhaps it's La Rocca. Towering above Cefalù, this is home to the Tempio di Diana, a Mesolithic structure that was adapted by the Greeks in the fifth century BC.

(L) The medieval town of Cefalù; (T) Fishing boats moored up; (B) A luminous golden ceiling mosaic of Christ in the Duomo

Aeolian Islands

Named after Aeolus, the Greek god who kept the winds he controlled shut tight in one of the islands' many caves, the seven Aeolian Islands are a UNESCO-designated volcanic archipelago located in the Tyrrhenian Sea off the north-eastern coast of Sicily. Rugged, with sparkling black-sand beaches and active craters, the seven so-called "pearls" serve an intoxicating mix of myth, chic bohemianism, and untamed Mediterranean nature. Each island has its own distinct character. While Stromboli and Vulcan smoulder with active volcanoes and offer visitors opportunities to wallow in warm mud baths, greener Salina is an excellent place to walk. Then there's Panarea. Something of a playground for the rich and famous, this is the smallest, prettiest and most expensive of the Aeolians. And despite being the biggest and most developed island, Lipari still has some beautiful, unspoiled areas and blissful waters.

(O) The path to Stromboli; (L) Lipari's cliffs;
(T) Panarea is a popular holiday destination

Mount Etna

(T) Colourful volcanic fountains around Mount Etna

A smoking volcano whose slopes have shaped the region's agriculture and mythology for centuries, Mount Etna dominates eastern Sicily, physically and imaginatively. From Taormina or Catania, the mountain is a constant presence, sometimes clear and snow-streaked, sometimes veiled by cloud, and sometimes billowing smoke high into the sky. Climbing towards the craters brings a harsher scene, and the bleak lava wilderness around Mount Etna's summit is one of Italy's most memorable landscapes. Curiously, the volcano's height is constantly shifting, depending on whether eruptions are constructive or destructive. Whatever its exact current height, Etna remains one of the world's biggest active volcanoes, and has been in an almost continual state of eruption for several decades, with the vineyards and citrus groves that flourish on its lower slopes showing the fertility that can follow nature's elementally destructive forces.

Taormina

Perched high on Monte Tauro, overlooking two sweeping bays, with Mount Etna as a backdrop, Taormina might just be too enchanting for its own good. In fact, D.H. Lawrence was so enraptured by the town that he lived here from 1920–23. One of Italy's great natural theatrical compositions, Taormina's terraces and lanes seem as if they were deliberately designed for maximum effect. Its ancient Greek theatre, close to where D.H. Lawrence lived, is Taormina's defining sight, not only for its surviving stone auditorium, but also for the view beyond the stage, where sea, coast and volcano create a backdrop no set designer could possibly improve. Although international tourism has taken its toll on the town, Taormina remains ravishingly charming, speckled with small, intimate piazzas, and a traffic-free main street that presents an unbroken line of fifteenth- to nineteenth-century palazzi bedecked with fragrant flower-filled balconies.

(L) Taormina's ancient Greek theatre; (T) Café life; (B) Isola Bella is connected to Taormina by a narrow path

Siracusa & Ortigia

Under ancient Greek rule, Siracusa was the most important city in the Western world, and a sense of that status lingers to this day. Its archaeological area, Parco Archeologico della Neapolis, preserves an ancient theatre, where classical dramas are still staged in the vicinity of remains that recall the site's ancient power. Beyond the mainland, yet more riches are to be found on Ortigia Island. Resembling a fist of land with the thumb downturned, it somehow packs more than 2,700 years of history into a tiny space that's barely 1km long and 0.5km across. Connected to the mainland by two small bridges, this UNESCO-designated jewel is dense with piazzas, churches and palaces that encompass Greek, medieval and Baroque elements, often in a single building. Ortigia's awe-inspiring Baroque cathedral, for example, incorporates the elegant columns of a Greek temple into its more flamboyant later incarnation, thereby perfectly expressing the city's layered identity.

(O) Baroque fountains adorn Ortigia; (L) Looking down on Ortigia Island; (T) In Parco Archeologico della Neapolis; (B) Sunset-watching

Val di Noto

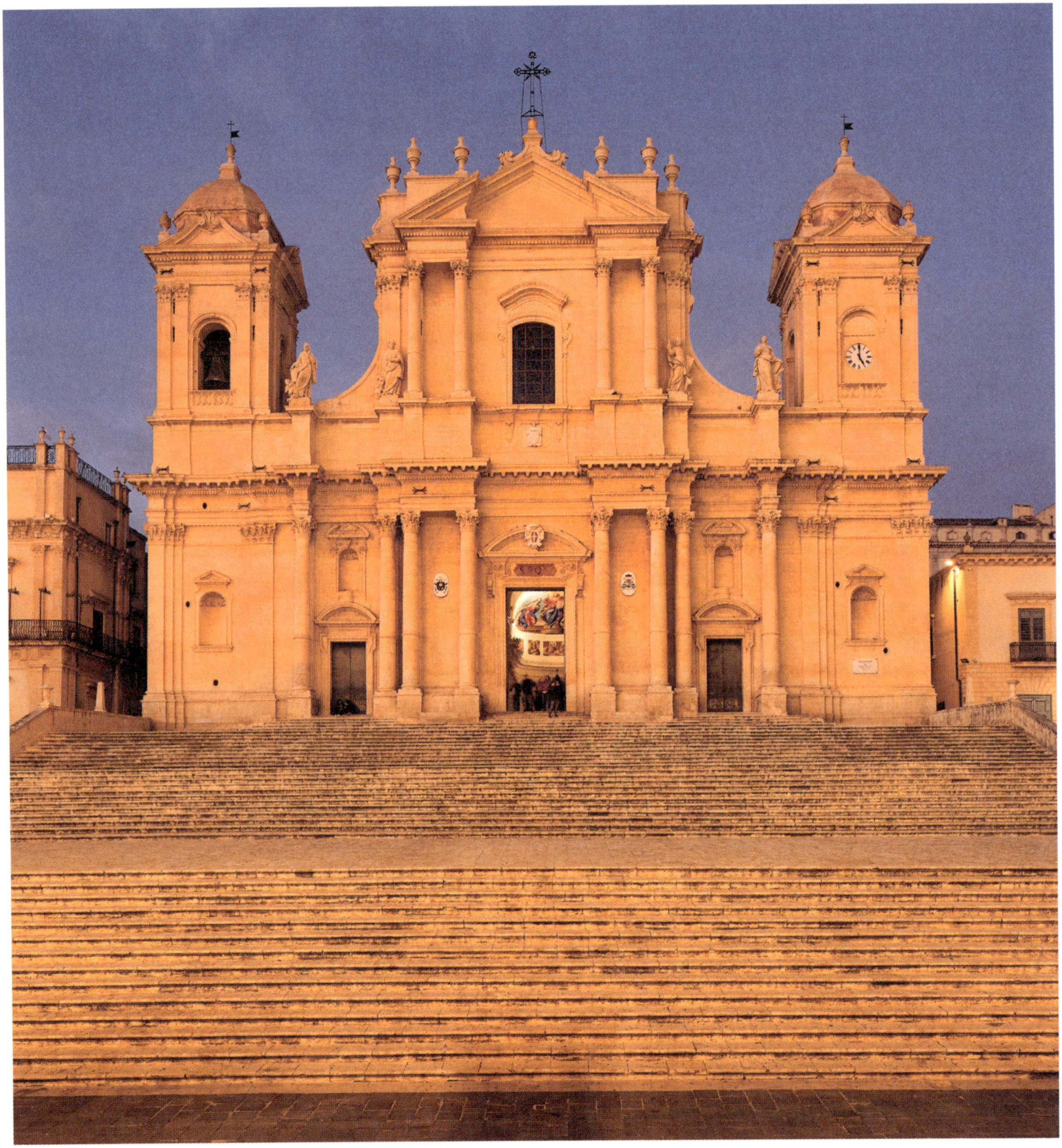

Characterized by warm, honey-hued limestone buildings, and grand cathedrals and palazzos, it's clear why the eight towns of south-eastern Sicily's Val di Noto have earned UNESCO World Heritage Site status. The reason for their existence is every bit as extraordinary as the towns themselves. After being struck by a devastating earthquake in 1693, the destroyed villages in this region were recast as meticulously planned towns to be rebuilt in an opulent Baroque style, with Noto arguably the most harmonious of the eight towns. Its main Corso is lined with some of Sicily's most captivating buildings, from the flat-fronted church of San Francesco, to the gracefully curving San Domenico. With its perfectly proportioned tree-planted expanses, Noto's Piazza Municipio is one of Sicily's finest piazzas, while its Duomo represents Baroque elegance in its most muscular form, with a couple of Michelin-starred restaurants further enhancing its elevated atmosphere.

(L) Noto's Basilica Minore di San Nicolò; (T) Palazzo Ducezio; (B) Baroque mascarons on the balconies

Valley OF THE Temples, Agrigento

One of the great survivors of the ancient Greek world, the architectural marvels of the Valley of the Temples stand on a ridge in southern Sicily. While the name is misleading, as the temples occupy high ground, the site's impact is beyond dispute. The history of the area stems back to 581 BC, when colonists founded the city of Akragas and surrounded it with a mighty wall, partly formed on a higher ridge that is today occupied by the modern town. At the southern limit of the ancient city was a lower ridge, and it was here, in the "Valle dei Templi", that architects erected their sacred buildings in the fifth century BC. Today, a road winds down from the modern city to the two-zoned Valle dei Templi. While the most immediately spectacular remains are in the eastern area, the western side offers a greater sense of discovery and holds the lovely gardens of Kolymbetra.

(O) Looking out over the Valley of the Temples; (L) Temple of the Dioscuri in the Valley of the Temples; (T) Evocative ruins

Sardinia

Across the Tyrrhenian, glittering Sardinia keeps its distance. Cagliari's Castello looks out over the harbour, lagoon and dry southern hills, while Nora and Su Nuraxi trace the island's story from ancient civilisations to the unique prehistoric Nuragic culture. Alghero brings Catalan echoes to the northwest coast, La Pelosa dazzles beside Stintino, and Tiscali draws the journey inland to limestone mountains, hidden caves and the mysterious stone remains of an ancient settlement.

Cagliari Castello

(T) Cagliari's coastal skyline

Cagliari's Castello quarter showcases the Sardinian capital at its most atmospheric. A walled hilltop district of narrow lanes, hardy bastions and old palazzi, this is the medieval heart of a city described by English novelist D.H. Lawrence as "strange and rather wonderful, not a bit like Italy". Known locally as Casteddu, the Castello quarter was traditionally the seat of the administration, aristocracy and highest ecclesiastical offices. The most evocative entry point is the monumental late nineteenth-century Bastione di Saint Remy, which rises from Piazza Costituzione. At the top of the grandiose flight of steps inside the bastion, Cagliari's best views over the port, and the lagoons beyond, are there for the taking. Lying either side of the city, the lagoons provide important habitats for cranes, cormorants and flamingos. While the quarter has an elevated character, small churches, museums and residential streets give it a real sense of local life beyond the postcard views.

Nora

Set on a low promontory near the sea, the ancient remains of Nora constitute one of Sardinia's most important and evocative archaeological sites. While much of the old town is submerged, what survives is enough to suggest its former importance. Founded by the Phoenicians and later settled by the Carthaginians and Romans, Nora was abandoned around the third century AD, possibly as a result of a natural disaster. The remains visible today include houses, Carthaginian warehouses, a temple, and baths, with well-preserved mosaics scattered around the site, especially in the House of the Tetrastyle Atrium, where a depiction of a Nereid nymph riding a sea creature sits at the centre of detailed geometric designs. In addition, Nora's Roman amphitheatre still hosts performances through the summer months. Unlike inland archaeological sites, Nora feels exposed to the Mediterranean that shaped it, with waves and light altering its mood throughout the day and across the seasons. Sunsets here are exceptional.

(L) The Spanish Coltellazzo of Saint Efisio lighthouse; (T) Nora extends into the sea; (B) Bright sea, brooding backdrop

Su Nuraxi

Su Nuraxi is the most compelling example of Sardinia's indigenous Bronze Age Nuraghic civilization, the mark of which is seen through thousands of circular defensive towers *(nuraghi)* scattered across the island. Located in Barumini, and surrounded by the bronzed hills of Sardinia's interior, this UNESCO-protected site is the largest and oldest Nuraghic complex on the island. Thought to date from around 1500 BC, it was unearthed in 1949 after a torrential rainstorm. At its centre stands a huge tower with three chambers (the uppermost has been lost) connected by a spiral staircase. Around this, four secondary towers are linked by a massive stone wall, creating a courtyard that limits access to the central stronghold. Unique to Sardinia, *nuraghi* are thought to have first been built by kin groups or clans, with more buildings added as Nuraghic society became more complex, as appears to be the case at Su Nuraxi, where the remains of a settlement of circular huts sit beyond the quadrant of towers.

(O) The ancient megalithic fortress of Su Nuraxi; (L) In the archaological site; (T) Tour groups exploring; (B) In the ruins

Alghero

A busy but charming resort town, Alghero's old centre exudes a distinctly Catalan flavour from centuries of Spanish rule. So thorough was the process of Hispanicization that the town became known as "Barcelonetta". Today, the flamboyant churches and cobbled lanes of Alghero's old quarter are named in both Italian and Catalan, with the Palazzo d'Albis and elegantly austere Palazzo Carcassona (now a restaurant) two of the best examples of the Catalan-Gothic style that characterises Alghero's finest architecture. Another old quarter highlight is the circuit of seven defensive towers. Located on the southern seawall, the octagonal Torre di San Giacomo (Tower of the Dogs) serves unobstructed panoramic sea views. Beneath the heights of the old town is a busy port, with the Riviera del Corallo coastline, known for its beautiful beaches and red coral, stretching from Alghero to Capo Caccia. Another notable local natural attraction is the Grotta di Nettuno, an immense sea cavern complex accessed by boat, or by descending the cliffside Escala del Cabirol stairway.

(L) A colourful door in Alghero; (T) Alghero's townscape; (B) The protected marine natural area of Capo Caccia

La Pelosa & Stintino

A small, laidback fishing village for most of the year, Stintino shifts into a busy resort destination through the summer months as a result of its proximity to outstanding beaches, with La Pelosa the most lauded of them all. Looking out to the islets of Piana and Asinara, and overlooked by the sixteenth-century Aragonese watchtower, the pale, powdery sand and dazzlingly turquoise waters are more evocative of the tropical Caribbean than of Europe. Unsurprisingly, La Pelosa attracts large numbers through the summer, but it's true to say that nothing can dampen the soul-stirring joy of its setting. Asinara Island is another highlight. Formerly a leper colony, later a prison, and now a national park, it can be reached by a public ferry service or as part of a boat trip. Wild-feeling on land, and home to wild boars and the white Asinara donkey, among many other species, Asinara is surrounded by a pristine marine reserve.

(O) The boardwalk to possibly the most beautiful beach in Sardinia, La Pelosa; (L) Sailing over crystal clear waters; (T) La Pelosa's white sands, backed by bright green foliage

Tiscali

Spectacularly sited within a vast mountaintop cavern, within a vast sinkhole, the Nuraghic village of Tiscali is one of Sardinia's most rewarding archaeological sites. Reached by trekking some of the island's most rugged interior terrain, in part along age-old shepherding paths, it also offers one of the island's best hikes. Invisible from the outside, the site comprises two complexes of around 100 Bronze Age dwellings, some circular, others four-cornered, with a clutch making direct use of the cave walls. Though built by Sardinia's indigenous Nuraghic people, archaeological digs have unearthed Roman material as well as Nuragic items, including jars, cups, and decorated jugs. Some scholars argue that the site's second set of dwellings indicates that Tiscali was occupied much later still, perhaps through to the late Medieval period. Entirely different in character and form from all currently known Nuraghic sites, Tiscali's sense of mystery is enhanced by its otherworldly setting: scrubland and craggy, stark-white karst broken by big skies and brilliant green foliage.

(L) In the Nuragic site of Tiscali

Publishing information

Italy • 100 Legendary Places
Editor: Sarah Clark
Proofreader: Siobhan Warwicker
Designer: Michał Ptasznik
Picture Editor: Piotr Kala
Picture Manager: Tom Smyth
Production Operations Manager: Katie Bennett
Publishing Technology Manager: Rebeka Davies
Head of Publishing: Sarah Clark

Our selection
Italy • 100 Legendary Places offers our curation of the most exceptional destinations in the country, with choices and content based on *Rough Guides Italy*. The most recent edition of *Rough Guides Italy* was updated by Ros Belford.

First Edition 2026

ISBN: 9781835297759

Printed by Finidr in Czech Republic

A catalogue record for this book is available from the British Library.

Distribution
UK, Ireland and Europe
Apa Publications (UK) Ltd; mail@roughguides.com
United States and Canada
Two Rivers; ips@ ingramcontent.com
Australia and New Zealand
Woodslane; info@woodslane.com.au
Worldwide
Apa Publications (UK) Ltd; mail@roughguides.com

Special Sales, Content Licensing and CoPublishing
Rough Guides can be purchased in bulk quantities at discounted prices. We can create special editions, personalized jackets and corporate imprints tailored to your needs.
mail@roughguides.com; http://roughguides.com

EU Representative
LOGOS EUROPE, 9 rue Nicolas Poussin, 17000, LA ROCHELLE, France
Contact@logoseurope.eu; +33 (0) 667937378

Photo credits

All images Shutterstock except:
Adobe Stock 90
Alamy 152/153, 200/201

Cover credit: Atrani on the Amalfi Coast **iStock**

Caption key
(L) = left
(R) = right
(T) = top
(B) = bottom
(O) = opposite